HOPE IS HERE

An Anthology of Testimonies

Craig
I hope that you enjoy this book as much as I did. Thank you for your support
Agnes Gross

THE VISION TO FRUITION GROUP

Hope Is Here

An Anthology of Testimonies

Presented by

The Remnant of Hope International Church

Hope Is Here: An Anthology of Testimonies

ISBN: 978-1-7358359-0-7

Cover Design Collaboration by The Vision to Fruition Group and LCB Enterprises, LLC d.b.a. Consulting and Design

Editing and Layout by LCB Consulting and Design
www.consultLatricia.com

The Vision to Fruition Publishing House
www.vision-fruition.com

PRINTED IN THE U.S.A.

ENDORSEMENTS

The anthology, 'Hope, Is Here' is must-read. Anyone who breathes upon the earth can connect to the heart of each writer as they take us through a channel of their life. The testimonies are relative and relational, revealing how God can turn potential ruin into revival. I believe this anthology is a vaccine for those who find themselves in hopeless arenas of life. This book is more than consonants and vowels, it is hope in present form.

❖ PASTOR MICHAEL P. BARBER, Senior Pastor, Dominion Apostolic Ministries International

HOPE IS HERE: An Anthology of Testimonies is expressions of life experiences that describe a level of truth that grabs the attention of the reader. The vulnerability of these testimonies causes the reader to identify with their own personal areas of struggle and victories. Through a raw and relatable display of emotions and life events, the reader can feel the author's experience. These relatable testimonies will leave you in awe, feeling empowered and most of all—HOPEFUL. This book is a must-read that will transform and impact lives through the power of one's testimony.

❖ DR. SHAKINA DUNBAR RAWLINGS, Pastor, Kingdom Fellowship Church

Hope Is Here is a compilation of compelling testimonies of God's love, grace, and transforming power. The transparency of the authors is thought-provoking and inspiring. The hand of God is made visible as each writer shares their personal and intimate journey with the Lord. The readers will be encouraged and strengthened as they experience the authenticity of the authors' diverse encounters with God. Hope Is Here, personifies the scripture: "God is our refuge and strength, a very present help in trouble (Psalm 46:1 KJV)."

❖ BISHOP STEPHANIE STRATFORD, D. Min., Ekklesia International

DEDICATION

To everyone who needs HOPE, it is HERE!

TABLE OF CONTENTS

FOREWARD

We are often blessed to cross paths with individuals who have a unique ability to face life with a grace and demeanor that demands admiration. Pastor Margo Gross is one of those individuals.

I have known Margo since she was a teenager. She grew up with my children. Even then I saw something unique in her. She was bold, outspoken, and daring. She had a determination to push through obstacles that stood in her way. Time went on, and we reconnected. I was so excited to see how she had grown up and become a beautiful and intelligent woman of God.

As I sat in my office one day in a meeting with this poised woman of God, it made me pose the question, "Who are you in God that I should know you?" As she shared the things in life that made her into the woman of God that I have witnessed, it became clear to me that this is a gift that will soon leave an indelible mark in the Kingdom of God. The anointing for ministry just seemed to ooze from her. Pastor Margo Gross finds expression as a five-fold ministry teacher, exhorter, encourager, mentor, pastor and now an author. Her life echoes passion and conviction. She has a uniqueness about her that drives others to be their best. She wants to see them succeed in everyday life, to overcome obstacles, to love themselves, have a relationship with God, and walk out their purpose and destiny! She has been a tireless advocate for helping people overcome their problems in real life, wherein I am so honored to recommend this book that will bring hope to so many.

As I was reading these testimonies in this book, I just knew in my heart that whoever reads it will be helped because these are real life situations, with real people that overcame. There are people waiting for a book like this. I am happy to have contemplated truth, weighed issues, and shared deep revelations with such a mighty people of God. Further, I am honored to have my life intersect with Pastor Margo's at this pivotal moment in her ministry. This is truly a defining moment in the life of gifted vessels of God. It is with conviction that this book is not just ink on paper, but it is the revealing of a God who delivers and sets free. There are those who are blessed to share their experience, and those who read them will be inspired by the triumphant outcome.

This book is designed to be a beacon of hope and a call to a deeper relationship with God the Father.

Bishop Bonnie Hunter
Senior Pastor, Friendship Church Outreach Ministry, Inc.
Founder of Kingdom Fellowship of Churches, Inc.

PREFACE

I, too, have experience with the quest to hold on to hope. Abandoned as a child, growing up surrounded with addiction and domestic violence, illiterate, overcoming infidelity, self-worth issues, and the grief of losing loved ones have all been elements of my testimony. I have found the Holy Spirit to be a comforter. I have found Romans 5:1-5 KJV to be both true and comforting.

> *1 Therefore being justified by faith, we have peace with God through our Lord Jesus Christ: 2 By whom also we have access by faith into this grace wherein we stand, and rejoice in hope of the glory of God. 3 And not only so, but we glory in tribulations also: knowing that tribulation worketh patience; 4 And patience, experience; and experience, hope: 5 And hope maketh not ashamed; because the love of God is shed abroad in our hearts by the Holy Ghost which is given unto us.*

Our hope is not in this world. Our hope is not in our possessions, economic status, titles, or positions. Our hope is in God. He can show up and show off in the darkest of times. He can be the hope that brightens this world. Hope in God will never make us ashamed. We can never go wrong when we put our trust in God. Hold on to hope.

HOPE IS HERE!

INTRODUCTION

To put it simply, this book is for the hopeless—those who have stopped expecting a blessing. It is for people who have tried and failed often. It is for the broken man, the lonely woman. It is for the sick, wounded, and bruised. This book does not hold pretty stories of lives full of glamor and privilege. No, this book tells the raw truth about life. Truth that sometimes hits you in the face, messes with your mind, and seeks to devour your soul. These authors are not telling you about what they have read or heard. They are telling of the goodness of God that they have experienced to be true. These are their personal walks with God—uncut, real, raw, and relevant. As their testimonies come alive, so will you.

I know God wants this book to be a voice to the hopeless who cannot see the light for the darkness. He wants you to know that the sun will shine for you again just like it did for us. He wants you to be encouraged to stay in the fight for your life. His desire is that our testimonies help you to overcome. This book will change your perspective, shift your focus, and open your eyes to the hope that has been within your reach. When we speak of hope, we are not speaking of a mere wish. No, wishes will not do. This hope that you will find here is more than a wish. This hope is faith. It is earnest expectation that God has moved, is moving, and will move on your behalf. It is a hope that is not founded on people and things. It is all about the hope that is found through Jesus Christ.

This book is a revival. It is the AED (automated external defibrillator) for your life. This collection of testimonies addresses many of life's challenges and proves how God has given us the victory. Written by members of the Remnant of Hope International Church, this anthology features testimonies about overcoming:

- Divorce
- Abuse
- Addiction
- Fornication
- Being a Widow
- Cancer
- Daddy Issues
- Sickness
- A Broken Heart

A word of encouragement, Heap of Hope, comes after each testimony to elaborate on God's ability to restore you. Expect to be moved, encouraged, and revived as we agree with Revelations 12:11:

> *And they overcame him by the blood of the lamb,*
> *and by the word of their testimony; and they loved not*
> *their lives unto death.*

Margo Gross

"As Christians we are to repeat the story of God's love to others who need to hear it."

Senior Pastor

Margo Gross, Senior Pastor
Remnant of Hope International Church

I Still Kept Smiling

"A smile on a bad day speaks to our joy, faith, and hope in a brighter future."

by Trinity Clayton

I Still Kept Smiling

by Trinity Clayton

As a young child I was never afraid of the dark. I found it comforting. The silence, the space, the ability to let my imagination run free when I knew it was time to wind down for bed. I always looked forward to the things I would see in my dreams. As I got older, I started to get nightmares. Nothing scary—simple things like a bird chasing me, or my doll being stolen—nothing serious. As these nightmares continued, I became afraid of the dark. I was scared to dream and afraid to let my imagination free. After a while, I got a night light to keep me grounded. It was something to look at to keep my mind on one thing at a time.

Underage

I was exposed to a lot of things as a child: The underage drinking. Kids in the neighborhood doing drugs. People in the neighborhood killing each other for the simplest of things. At the time, I was too young to understand the underlying issue, so I shoved the memory of it all into the back of my mind and pretended like it never happened. I never knew what kind of hardship situation my family and I were in until Christmas came. I was taken to the local Walmart and was told to pick out two toys. After I had gone through the catalog of toys that was sent in the mail. I circled all the toys I wanted. Though I only got two, I kept smiling. I still never knew what kind of financial situation we were in even when we did not have electricity for about two days. Instead, I thought it was kind of fun—a game. It was not scary because I was with my family. The people who would protect me until the very end.

I was a dancer for the church I had attended most of my childhood. I loved dancing with my entire soul, and I thought of it as my outlet. I did not need to talk. I just had to dance, and people would understand how I was feeling. I recall one day this girl came up to me and asked, "Why are you always smiling? I see you everywhere, and all you do is smile." It left me speechless. I did not know what to say to her for a second. How did she notice I was smiling all the time? I had not fully processed what I was going through even after about a year since my parents got divorced. I did not even realize I was smiling when she asked me the question. I never even bothered to answer her.

My mom almost died one time when I was 8 years old. She had a small intestine blockage. It was terrifying because I did not know if mommy was going to come home. Today, I do not remember much of that day, except for the deep fear I had. The goosebumps I get when I think of that time haunt me to this day. My mom is the strongest woman I have ever known. When she talks about the incident to people, I cannot help but get a little teary. I start thinking about all the outcomes, the things that could have happened, and how none of them occurred. All I remember is looking at my nightlight and praying while I held my doll and I cried myself to sleep.

The next morning, I would check on my brother and dad, and see if they were okay. I would smile in their faces wanting to be the sunshine to their cloudy day.

My brother got caught up in a lot of stuff when he was in high school. I was still young at this time, so I sat and watched as he made money in his own unique way. I watched him do so many dumb things–the girls, the alcohol, and the drugs. My brother is a smart person, he just made dumb choices. One time he came home on Halloween with alcohol poisoning. I danced at a Halloween Party at my daycare center that day. So, imagine my disappointment when my dad did not come, nor did my brother. I was a few breaths from going to sleep when my brother walked in the house fumbling and stumbling down the hall into my room talking about the great party he went to. Then he went ahead into the bathroom and vomited his guts out. There are three things I simply cannot stomach: eyeballs, spit, and vomit. Our parents went into the bathroom and were trying to take care of him while they scolded him for being so irresponsible. Again, I watched my nightlight and prayed that night as I cried myself to sleep. The next morning, I went to my brother's room to see if he was okay. Thank God, he was.

Fifth Grade

We moved out of my neighborhood when I was entering the 5th grade. Nobody told me until a week before that we were moving about an hour or two away. I was quite sad because I did not want to leave my friends. Somewhere inside me I knew that when they said, "You can still come back and see them every now and again." I knew it was not true.

I saw this lady get beat up by her boyfriend one time. I was outside waiting for the bus stop with my brother and this guy just choked his girlfriend outright there in front of me. I was curious as to what she did to make him physically want to harm her since my brother and I were taught it is not polite to hit people. She kind of just stared at me as she was getting hit and choked. I was too young and too terrified to do anything, so I sent a prayer to God asking him to cover her. I gave her a thumbs up from where I was standing, and quietly walked away to tell my brother what I did.

My parents got divorced in the spring when I was in 5th grade. My brother was the one who told me. "You haven't seen mom wear her ring, have you?" That was the first time I experienced heartbreak. I knew couples had disagreements every now and then, but even at this age, I did not ever think my parents would break up. It sent me into a spiral. Why me? How could they? These things ran through my mind. There were so many emotions running through my head, I almost instantly became numb. I had to move to my grandmother's house with my mom, while my brother stayed with my dad. The moving process was hard because of the memories everything held. The view out my bedroom window, the dent in the wall, the stickers in my closet, everything. Despite all these changes, I kept smiling.

Middle School

Somewhere in middle school I got lost. I did not know who I was, and I went looking for an identity from anybody who would give me attention. I wanted to befriend anybody who gave me the slightest bit of acknowledgement. This was around the time I became aware of mental health. People I knew at this time had always made it seem like having mental health problems was cool and trendy. Girls would always use the term, "KMS" which is an abbreviation for "Kill Myself." They would use the term when something did not go their way. Some would also flaunt the fact that they went to psychologists and other mental health professionals. I wanted to fit in then. I wanted friends, and I wanted to be friends with the "popular" kids. I asked my mom for a therapist. I told her I needed one. Realistically, I did not, yet I kept smiling because I was one step closer to having friends.

Mom and I were on a constant church hunt after we moved out. We went to a new church every Sunday. None of them felt like they were for me. Nothing interested me, nothing made me want to stay. After a while we stopped looking. We gave up on the idea of church, letting the light we so desperately wanted to hold onto, dim out. I still slept with a light on and my smile sometimes faltered. I looked up at the sky a lot at night. Just looking, sometimes thinking: "Why me? Why did we have to be in this position? When is God going to give us a miracle?" Once again, I would shed tears and not sleep until 1 a.m. These thoughts always appeared at night. Sadly, I never got a response. Eventhough I waited on a miracle, I still smiled in everyone's faces like nothing ever happened.

Freshman Year

Freshman year I began getting into fashion—choosing what colors to mix; what patterns to incorporate; what style I wanted for the specific day. I even chose which persona I wanted to be for that specific day. I soon found myself with a friend group. These people would stick with me forever, I thought. We talked all day and texted all night. We made plans to do so much when we got older. We planned trips, had sleepovers, we were even going to make a joint YouTube channel together. We had our little arguments here and there, of course, but they were never so bad that they could not be fixed the next day.

When my mom started getting out and dating again, it was quite the process. Her first boyfriend was a devious guy. When my mom told me she broke it off, I was curious as to why. She refused to tell me, but I found out he cheated. I just felt bad. Why did all these things happen to my mom when she did nothing but try to help everybody she met? I thought the second guy, a musician, would last a while. Had an in-home studio. He even had a few daughters, and I became friends with them. Since he had a studio, I made cute little songs with his daughter. We had fun! Then he started lying to my mom about what he was doing, or who he was doing. So, she ended that. I remember one day when she met my dad to pick me up, we talked about what had happened, and we cried. We both thought he would have been the last. Watching my mom get hurt back to back like that really hurt me. These men who promised my mom the world gave her nothing but added pain to her already established problems. These men who promised me happiness and fortune lied to me. I put on a brave face for my mom, because at the end of the day, we still had each other.

We finally found a new church. There were some familiar faces in the congregation, and it had this welcoming feeling. Originally, I was not too fond of being there, because we had been out of church for so long. I was not fond of waking up early on a Sunday to go hear a crowd of people yelling and screaming. But it was not like that at all. It was calm, and even when the Pastor had a message, she got it across without the organ playing for added drama effect. I started going to this church every Sunday without thinking much of it. Then about after the fifth time, my mom decided we should join. I did not think I would have met so many kind and real people at the church I am at now. More importantly, my bond with God is greater than it was 10 years ago.

Sophomore Year

Towards the end of sophomore year, I felt like I feared change. I was afraid that if I made a big change, I would be alone. I thought I would not have anybody to back me up or help me through the change. But as I moved forward, I realized I would rather have a select few people in my corner then have many people I call friends putting me down and telling me things I can and can't do. So, I made the change. I broke things off with all my friends sophomore year. I felt like they were not good for me. Maybe I wasn't good for them. Who really knows? I loved them just as they loved me, but things were not moving in a good direction. I had things I needed to work on as a person, and I could not do them when I was being doubted constantly. They would not have been able to be genuinely happy with me being the way I was back then, and it was okay. Even when I cried and yelled at them in the middle of the hallway, I still smiled, because I knew I was finally free to do whatever I wanted to. At least I thought so. Anxiety and depression are something I would never wish on my worst enemy. My depression moved slowly and quietly. It was a subtle feeling of disinterest in everything. I tried to isolate myself from everyone. At the time it felt okay until I wanted to go out in public and I could not talk to a cashier or a store worker alone without my mom there with me. I could not do anything for myself.

Junior Year

I started junior year fresh. I had acquaintances around the school and people I met and befriended during the summer. But somewhere early in the beginning of school, I stopped genuinely smiling. I wanted to be transparent. I wanted to let myself feel and be free. So as my façade began to fade. I was getting worse and worse at hiding my own build-ups. It was getting harder to hold onto all the issues inside me without crying daily to my mom or sitting in the shower blank faced. I had thousands of thoughts at a second. I stopped going to church for a while. My mind was not in the right place and it felt like everything was crashing down. I even missed school for two days. I could not understand why I felt like everything was hitting me at once, and it just seemed like I could not escape my own mind. I tried aromatherapy, essential oils, even music. Nothing worked. I tried blocking everything out. That only made it worse, and on top of that I started getting these heart palpitations. The first time I had one I thought I was having a heart attack and I was dying. I was home alone, and I would not stop crying. I had to call my mom and listen to her voice to calm me completely down. This went on for days. Days turned to weeks; weeks turned to months. My mental state did not get any better and every little thing was stressing me out. The heart palpitations happened daily, and I cried every night. It got so bad one night I went to the hospital at 1 a.m. with chest pains and a heart rate of 120. I genuinely thought I was gonna die. Once I got there they tested, my heart and my lungs. Nothing was wrong with me. When I calmed down, the pain went away, and my heartbeat slowed. I later found out that it was an anxiety attack that day.

I wanted to be the best. I wanted to be the best at everything I did and if I were not good at it, I would quit. For a while I thought of myself figuratively as a reset button. My brother did not take the path everybody wanted him to go down, so I felt as if the pressure was put on me to be the greatest. Nobody in my immediate family went to college. So, I felt like all that pressure would sink onto me. It was a lot of pressure. Mainly because I did not know what I wanted to do in the future. I felt as if I would not have been someone to be proud of if I did not get a job that required the mind of an intellectual scholar.

Comfort in the Dark

One night I asked God to show me what I was so afraid of. I turned off the light I usually keep on and I just sat there in the dark, letting the darkness comfort me. As the night lingered on, I started to see little things floating through my room—all the things I stressed about all night; everything I thought about throughout the day, floating around my room. I was not afraid of the dark. I was afraid of the dark thoughts my mind made up in the dark. That night, I prayed about everything. My dad, my brother, my mom, school, my job, my friends, everything. I fell asleep while I prayed. I woke up the next morning feeling different. I was smiling, but it was finally a real smile.

After that night, I talked to my mom. I opened up to her. I told her everything I had not told her years prior. I started with her divorce to my newly developed anxiety. I did not leave anything out. She understood me and how I felt. I ended up getting a doctor's opinion and was put on medication to help with my anxiety. I have not lied about my feelings to anybody anymore, I specialize in being truthful to everybody I cherish in my life. As I have lived my short seventeen years. The amount of people I have seen ruin themselves is unreal. I feel like I have grown to where I can be confident in my own skin. I can be proud of my heritage. I can be grateful for the things I have seen and heard for shaping me into the person I am today. I am thankful to God for giving me the strength to get through this and other things that were not mentioned here. I was told a while ago from Pastor, that I feel my way through life using my sensitivity. And I do believe that when I finally embraced this concept, I became a better me. Once I realized the lie about the statement, "failure is not an option," I was able to allow myself to fail a few times without breaking down. I realized, instead, to learn from the failures, and not make the same mistakes again.

Pastor Margo's Heap of Hope

Smile! Many do not understand the impact of a smile. At times, our soul and face do not walk in agreement. Our smile can serve as a form of warfare, confusing the enemy. A smile on a bad day speaks to our joy, faith, and hope in a brighter future. It is not phony or fake to smile through adversity. It does not mean the problem has been eliminated or trouble has not hit our front door. Our unconditional smile simply means we trust God enough to know that even in the worst of times we know that all things are working for our good. (Romans 8:28 KJV)

Proverbs 17:22 tells us, "A merry heart doeth good like a medicine." So, throw your head back, laugh at the inevitable defeat of the enemy, smack your thigh, and smile. Let your face speak to your absolute victory until your eyes (vision) align with your lips (smile). Then just SMILE!

Trinity Clayton Bio

Trinity Amour Clayton was born on March 8, 2003, in St. Mary's County, Maryland, to Suzanne (Clayton) Middleton and Timothy Clayton. Her one and only sibling is her older brother, DaJour Clayton.

Trinity, currently a junior attending Calvert High School, enjoys taking photos, giving people advice, and sleeping whenever she can. Trinity is an avid student enrolled in Advanced Honors and AP classes, and pursuing the field of nursing. She is college-bound, has great aspirations.

Trinity has been a member of Remnant of Hope International Church since 2017. She is an active member of the youth group, "The C.R.E.W."

Contact Me:

Web: https://bit.ly/trinityclayton

You Shall Live and Not Die

"Hope is here. I lived through it, and I did not die."

by Suzanne Middleton

You Shall Live and Not Die

by Suzanne Middleton

It was a Friday evening after a long day at work. I went out to dinner with my family. We decided to go to Outback Steakhouse for dinner. We ordered bread, appetizers, and drinks. I was about five minutes into eating when suddenly I began having a sharp pain in my stomach. At times it was so sharp I had to hold my stomach to try making the pain stop. I sat there wondering what was going on. We realized something serious was going on with me by the time the main entrée made it to our table. The only thing I could do was look at it. Fifteen minutes went by, and the pain was getting worse. My family could see that I was in pain as I began to tear up. I mumbled to them that we needed to leave. By this time, not only was I starting to feel faint, I started to feel like I was going to regurgitate. When I stood up to put my jacket on, I realized I could not stand straight up. I had to walk out of the restaurant bending over. I got to the car and had no energy left. The ride home made me feel worse. I felt like I was being stabbed with a sharp knife with every bump we rode over. We finally made it to the garage at the house. I struggled as I forced myself to get out of the truck with help. This is when I realized I could not walk without assistance. "Oh my God!" I said. "What is happening to me?" The tears began flowing down my face. I literally thought I was going to die. "Please call for an ambulance for me!" I cried in constant pain. The fear of not knowing what was happening to me made me begin thinking about things only the devil would have me thinking at a time like this. "If I die, who's going to take care of my babies?" I thought.

I heard the siren from the ambulance outside. My sissy and best friend, Terra Holton, was on the phone, wondering what was wrong with me. This lady was sent by God to cover me. I believe our connection was truly a Godly, divine connection without doubt. Through the best and the worst of times, she has always been there for me. We have been best friend for about 30 years now. I was in so much pain I could not talk. I was a mess and so was my daughter, Trinity Amour. It was hard seeing her suffer, but even harder for me not to physically express how much pain I was in. My son, DaJour, tried his best to comfort her. I covered my face from the pain, the shame, and the embarrassment of what I was going through. The ride in the ambulance was worse than the ride in the car. The bumps in the road felt like we were rolling over potholes doing eighty miles per hour. The only thing I could do was cry. As my mind and spirit mentally uttered other languages for me.

When I got to the hospital in LaPlata, Maryland, I thought they would roll me straight to a bed in the emergency room. Instead, they put me in a wheelchair and rolled me out into the waiting room. How could they do this to me? I began moaning and the tears were flowing down non-stop. I continued crying, moaning, and groaning. I needed God, and I needed Him right away. I began speaking in tongues again and praying softly. If I ever needed the Lord to take away the excruciating pain, this was the time

I needed Him to do it. The pain was not going anywhere. It was there to stay. My name was finally called to go to triage after waiting for over twenty-five long minutes. While in triage, I could not answer the questions. The only thing I could do was moan. I said a silent prayer. Father, allow these people to see how much pain I am really in. Allow me to be next in line for help. Father take away the pain I feel I can no longer bear. Father, I need you to do a quick work now! Father, PLEASE HELP ME!!!! I continued to speak in tongues, and they wheeled me back to the waiting room. I complained to my heavenly Father by mumbling words in disgust. I was honestly asking Him to allow them to show me favor and take me back quickly. I did not want to be in pain for another second.

My name was finally called. The nurse began asking questions, but again, I was in too much pain to answer. Thankfully, there was someone with me who could answer the questions. Shortly after that they administered pain medication to me through an IV. I was lethargic. I could no longer moan, groan, or think. I laid still with my eyes closed. I wanted the pain to stop. By this time, Pastor Vince Williams came to check on me. He began praying for me while his wife Monika interceded at home. Shortly after, my bestie, Alicia Washington, and CeCe Mackall arrived. I knew they were there, and I heard them praying, but at the time I was in my quiet place and had no words to say. They could clearly see that the pain was great. My focus was on one thing and one thing alone. I waited patiently. I began to feel the pain subside. Finally, I was in a place of pure solace. I was able to open my eyes and thank them for coming and praying for me.

I stayed in the hospital overnight while the doctor ran several tests to figure out what was going on with me. My mom and sister, Victoria, ended their trip early to come see me. My sister, Roxanne, came with them to the hospital the next day. I had no answers for them as to what was going on with me. I noticed by the second day that my stomach looked as if I were about five or six months pregnant. I could not eat anything solid, so the only thing I had to eat during this time was crushed ice. The nurse came in to tell me that I was going to be discharged. "Discharged!" I said in disbelief. "Why would you discharge me not knowing what's going on with me? Look at my stomach. You're still going to discharge me?" I asked again. "Yes," she said. The doctor said everything came back negative. They gave me a few prescriptions and I was on my way. I was shocked that they did not diagnose me with the reason for my pain and upset that it was plain to see that they did not even care.

One day later the same pain in my stomach came back again. This lasted for hours before I decided to go to the hospital. This time I decided to go to the hospital in Calvert County, in hopes of them finding out something. This trip to the hospital caused me to be admitted for a few more days and have yet another undiagnosed problem. I left the hospital feeling bad. I got home and started to get undressed. I started to feel worse as time went by. I tried to eat to see if that would make me feel better. This time I could not keep anything down. Not even water. And when I did not have any water left in my stomach to regurgitate, I started to dry heave. I felt the need to just lay down. At that instant, I heard the Holy Spirit plainly say to me, "Dee, if you lay here, you are going to die here." I forced myself to get up. I called my doctor and left a message for my doctor. She called me right away. I told her about the trips to the hospitals, the diagnosis the hospital gave me, and I shared with her how much pain I was currently in. She said there is no way it could possibly be that, especially with the pain you are having. She said I want you to come back to the hospital right away. I will let the doctors in the emergency room know that you are on your way. I had to bend over because of the pain as I got off the bed to dress myself. I had to head back to the hospital for the third time. It took me thirty minutes to dress myself because of the pain I was in. I was living in Charles County and it took about thirty-five minutes to get to the hospital. By the time we got off Route 235 to get onto Route 231, I thought I was going to die. 911 had to be called to meet me at the gas station after crossing the bridge on the Calvert side. I could not believe what was happening to me. The thought flashed in my mind again. Who is going to take care of my babies? Trinity was eight years old at the time and DaJour was sixteen, but they were still my babies, and I was worried for them. I felt like I was slipping away fast.

The ambulance got there about two minutes after we parked. They helped me out of the car onto the gurney. Off we went to the hospital. They asked questions while we were in route to the hospital. With my eyes closed, I tried my best to answer what I could, when I could. The pain was getting to be unbearable once again. I shut myself off to the world again. I remember crying and hearing my inner self saying, let them figure it all out themselves. I remember them saying, she is not answering any questions.

My mother comes in the emergency room with the fire of God in her hands. She anointed my head and my stomach with her oil and began to pray for me. Out of everything she said. I remember her saying, "Enough is enough!" When they take her back in this time, let them find exactly what is going on with her. I remember her rubbing my back. Her hands were so hot it made my body hurt even more. It was a kind of heat that I had never felt before. After she rubbed me for about five minutes, I had to finally say to her, "Please stop. It's hurting me."

The first dose of medication they gave me did not work. They then gave me Morphine, but my stomach could not take it, so I threw it all up. The third dose of medication they gave me worked and the pain started to finally go away. The next day they took test, after test, after test. They finally came up with my problem. My small intestine was blocked. This was the reason why I could not eat or drink anything without it coming back up. And this was also the reason why I looked like I was six months pregnant.

Shortly after the diagnosis, the nurse came in to tell me that they must do a Nasogastric Intubation. At first, I was thinking it was something simple. When she told me that she had to put a big tube in to my nose and down into my stomach to remove the waste. I told her she was not going to do that on me especially after showing me how long the tube was. I insisted that I was not going to let them put the long plastic tube up in my nose down into my stomach. She kept insisting that it was not going to be as bad as it may seem to be. I still was not convinced. Low and behold, I got up enough nerve for her to finally do it. I thought I was going to lose my mind. I kept saying, "Stop! Stop! Stop!" And yes, she had to stop because the tube was too big for my nose. She had to get the tube for children. This time it was successful. This was not a good feeling. A tube was running up through my nose, down my throat, and down into my stomach. I remember grabbing the nurse's hand. It did not seem like she was ever going to stop pushing it down to my stomach. She finally stopped. She attached the end of the tube to a canister and turned it on to start suctioning the waste out my stomach. Immediately the waste started to come through the tube and go into the canister. How disgusting! I thought about how I could have died from this. If I had not listened to the small, still voice of God telling me if I didn't get out of the bed and go back to the hospital right now, I would die, right there. I thank God I listened and went.

It was so irritating to talk and swallow with the tube in my throat. My throat was sore and dry because of the tube. I started to think about the sacrifices Jesus made for me, and the fight He fought for the sins of the world. After being whipped, He had to carry His own cross to Calvary where He suffered, bled, and died. Then I realized that my situation could not amount to what Jesus had to go through, so I began to speak life. My cousin Angel stopped by, along with my Aunts: Rosie, Mary, Evelyn, and Dolline; and my Uncles Cliff and Timmy. There were days I was discouraged and sad. So many days I was there alone looking at the four walls of the hospital room. I was having a pity party with myself. I questioned God and wanted answers to why I had to go through this situation feeling alone. I felt like no one cared, and I began to feel abandoned. One Wednesday night around 7:30 p.m., I remembered it was Bible Study night where I attended church at that time. I turned off the TV and began to weep uncontrollably. In walked my bestie, Alicia Washington, and Melvenna "Momma" Thompson. They took time out from Bible Study to come have prayer with me. When they walked in, they walked in with power and authority. I could not talk. I wept, and they prayed. Oh, my goodness, did they pray. When they began to pray, the waste flowing thru my tube began to turn a white clear color. I was being purged of all the negative thoughts and feelings I was going through. I was being healed. I thought about a red crimson that only Jesus could wash white as snow. I thought about the brown and black cows eating green grass, but their milk is white as snow. I had to ask for forgiveness. This was a part of God's work He was doing within me. This time alone was important to Him. He knows what is best even when I do not. I was so overwhelmed with love and the presence of God in my room. After the prayer I could only say, "Thank You." There were no other words I could think to say. In that moment, I knew I was rescued because of their obedience and sacrifice. After having the tube down my throat for two days, they finally removed the tube. They removed two whole canisters and a quart of waste from me. I could not believe it. God Kept Me!

Just when I thought this was all over and I was on the road to recovery, the enemy attacked me again after day six of being in the hospital. I remember going into the bathroom and looking at myself in the mirror. I did not recognize myself. So many things were going through my head. I began to speak life by saying, "You shall live, and not die." I kept repeating it to myself. I began trying to figure this thing out on my own. I shared my thoughts with my sissy, Terra, and Jane Washington, who kept me lifted daily on the prayer line that Prophet Donald Clark facilitated, and Prophetess Myra Patterson-Stewart often joined in on. Trust me, I was covered in prayer through the whole ordeal.

I remembered while sleeping that night, my body starting to shake uncontrollably. Then I saw a light at the top of what appeared to be some type of a tunnel I was floating in. My body was flying at a fast rate of speed up towards the light. While traveling towards the light, I remember hearing the high speed of wind in my ears as I was ascending higher and higher through this tunnel. I began to hear others that were traveling with me. I could not see the people, but I could feel their presence, and I could hear them. I am not sure if they were praying, talking, or mumbling in fear because of what we were experiencing at the time. I could not understand because of the wind in my ears. I was getting closer to the light that was bright. When I got to the top, I saw what appeared to be a mansion. The colors seemed as if they were alive and more beautiful and radiant than any colors I have ever seen on earth. My attention was drawn and being pulled to a window in this mansion I saw. When I looked at the person in the window. I noticed that it was my father, Joseph Lloyd Middleton, a.k.a. "Cornbread." He was standing in the window. I looked at him long enough to see his face. His face looked flawless, as if his life had taken him back to his thirties. It was then when I realized what was happening to me. My spirit had left my body, and I was in heaven.

I immediately took my focus away from daddy. My focus was on going back where I came from. If we had made eye contact with each other perhaps I would have stayed there. I remember saying to him, "Daddy I love you, but I'm not ready yet. I have to go back to DaJour and Trinity. I have to take care of them. They need me. I want to see them grow up and have babies. I love you daddy, but I have to go back." I remembered saying those words a few times, but I would not look at him. The fast speed that took me to the top of the tunnel, began pulling me back down the tunnel. The sound of the wind was again in my ears. My spirit was then shaking and forced back into my body. Realizing what had happened, I began to cry and with a grateful heart, I Praised My God! I thanked Him for another chance.

The bed I was laying in was drenched as if someone poured water on it. I needed to get up, but I was not able to pull myself up. I pushed the button for the nurse to come in. I told her something just happened to me that I could not explain. She wanted to check my vitals. Then she started asking questions and wanted to know if I was a diabetic. I told her no. She left the room and began calling other nurses to my room. She said, "Are you sure you're not a diabetic and you've never been one in the past?" I said, "No. What's going on?" She said, "Your blood glucose count is thirteen and we are trying to figure out why you're not in a coma right now." There were four nurses in my room. They brought in a large tube of sugar water to put in my IV to get my blood levels up. They kept pricking my finger to check my blood levels every five minutes to make sure it was going up. The nurse told me I was lucky. I told her I was blessed, without shame. Thank You Jesus! He did it again. On day eight, I left the hospital with a new look on life. I left not being able to fit the clothes I went in with, but at least I walked out. I am forever grateful for another chance. I can see the beauty of God's hands from various perspectives. I was healed, delivered, and set free. I knew that one day, my tests would be testimonies to encourage, inspire, and to uplift others. Hope Is Here. I lived through trials, and I did not die. There's work for me to do. And, today I get to share my testimonies with millions.

Pastor Margo's Heap of Hope

Live! It is imperative that we as believers understand that the enemy comes to kill, steal, and destroy (John 10:8-10). His assignment is not to just disrupt, frustrate, or get in the way. He desires to sift us as wheat (Luke 22:31). Sifting wheat took time back in Biblical times. The wheat had to be gathered and beaten to separate the grain from the stalk. Then the mixture was tossed in the air keeping what should be kept falling to the ground while everything else blew away. At last, the sifting occurred to remove undesired materials. However, Satan's plan is to send us through a process that leaves us broken, destroyed, and dead (physically and spiritually). There is good news. Jesus has a plan far greater than the enemies. He came that we might have life and have it more abundantly (John 10:10). His plan is not just for you to live, but to live in abundance. Our God is in the business of giving you the ability to live your best life and have access to everything He promised. As David reminds us, you shall not die, but LIVE, and declare the works of the Lord (Psalm 118:17)! Take life by the horns and live it in fullness knowing that you serve a God who died so that you could live.

Suzanne Middleton Bio

Suzanne Middleton was born on July 10, 1969 to the late Joseph "Cornbread" Middleton and Susie Parker Middleton. She is the proud mother of DaJour Alexander Clayton and Trinity Amour Clayton. She is the proud grandmother of Voisier Alphonzio Clayton, and Naisier Amir Clayton. Suzanne has four sisters, Roxanne Fletcher, Victoria Middleton, Lynn Middleton, and her beloved sister Laura Middleton, who passed before she had the opportunity to meet her.

Suzanne Middleton was ordained as a Minister in 2014, then joined The Remnant of Hope International Church in October of 2017. She currently sings with the Praise and Worship Team, and the Voices of Hope Church Choir, and serves on the Praise and Prayer Conference Committee.

Suzanne currently lives in Calvert County, Maryland, and enjoys taking out time to enjoy Gods creations. She also enjoys going to the beach, fishing, trying new restaurants, spending time with family, and her friends, including three of her closest friends—Terra Holton, Alicia

Washington and her first cousin, Angel Gray—whom she has been inseparable with since childhood. Suzanne also appreciates riding her motorcycle and taking landscape photographs. She is currently taking a photography training class with Tracey and DeVonna Franklin of Dream Life Visionz Photography. In addition to photography, Suzanne is planning on getting two or more books published in the future.

She is committed to saying, "Jesus is my first love, and He is the best thing that ever happened for me."

Contact Me:

Web: https://bit.ly/suzannemiddleton

Searching for a Father's Love

"God gives us countless opportunities to accept His gift."

by Vanessa Tyler-Gantt

Searching for a Father's Love

by Vanessa Tyler-Gantt

"Daddy come back. I miss you."

I remember calling out to an airplane flying overhead. My brother and I were in the backyard playing, and this was our custom every time we would see a plane. Although I have no recollection of being able to put a face to the title, I only knew that my faceless daddy was on an airplane somewhere headed to Turkey. We were too young to realize that our daddy was not on that airplane and too ignorant to know that even if he were, he would be unable to hear our cries. Of course, at that young age, I had no idea that I did have a father in heaven who heard my voice every time I cried out. A father who had been with me all the time. A father waiting to be acknowledged by me. A father I would discover later in my life.

One day my daddy did come back, just not the way I had imagined in my head. Instead of my daddy coming back to live with us, my daddy came for visits. There were times when we would go for visits to his house. We, being his five children. I am the fourth of five children born to my parents. I have three older sisters and one brother who is the baby of this clan. We would have weekend visits infrequently. It was during these visits that we were introduced to his female friends. Some we would only meet once since they did not stay around long, while others were around a little longer. Some were childless, but often these friends had children. If you are like me, you would think that a man with five kids of his own would have more than enough on his hands. However, my daddy did not think like me. Little did I know that my siblings and I would become the forgotten ones—the kids put on the back burner becoming secondary to these "new families" he created for himself. Even now I can remember him discussing in front of us the things he was doing with *them*. *Them* being the children that became his priority. It was during these times that seeds of resentment were being planted and would later be watered by his negligence toward us. Seeds of rejection and unworthiness would grow into something I could not quite explain. I wrestled with the thought that something was wrong with us, wrong with me. Perhaps that is why he always found women with kids, maybe they were better kids. Rejection coupled with abandonment was taking root and growing rapidly into a seething hate.

Even though my earliest memories are those of going to church five times a week, I was never taught that I had been fearfully and wonderfully made; or that I am a marvelous work created by a God of love. I cannot say with a hundred percent certainty that if I had this knowledge earlier on that it would have changed my teen years. Unfortunately, I will never know if it would have made these years any less turbulent. I went from wishing my daddy dead to threatening to kill my daddy with my own hands. If I could not have the daddy I wanted—the daddy I thought I surely deserved—then I would rather not have a daddy at all. How could

God have gotten this so wrong? We were always taught that God does not make mistakes, however in this instance I began to think that He had. At this point I no longer considered this man my daddy.

In retrospect, I am in no way proud of my behavior or my inability to control my emotions, emotions that began to control me. I now wonder just how many of my days have been cut short due to my blatant disrespect and dishonoring of my God-given father. Even after I became aware of the scripture Exodus 20:12 which says, "Honor thy father and thy mother: that thy days may be long upon the land which the LORD thy God giveth thee," I justified my behavior by calling my daddy a sperm donor and not a father, thereby negating its application in this situation. Even my play on words could not change the truth of God's Word. It is funny though how we try to manipulate scripture to fit our circumstance or need at the time. Talk about bending the truth.

There came a season when things mellowed out and there was peace all around. My mother instituted family dinners on Sundays after church, and we would all gather around the dining room table for good food and conversation. My daddy would bring the newspaper and read until dinner was ready and afterwards take a nap before going home. There were holidays and birthday celebrations spent together as a family. My daddy and I bonded over our shared love of all foods hot and spicy. Sometimes we would sit with a box of tissue between us as we enjoyed one fire-infused food after another. There were trips to Maryland to attend a wedding or visit family. Some of these trips were made with just my daddy and me. When we suffered the first loss in our immediate family, it was my dad who orchestrated a family-bonding trip.

When My girls were born, my daddy became a present and continually active granddad in their lives. He would load car seats and take them on trips to the park, circus, and zoo. These were his moments with his grandkids. More than once I would wonder where *THIS* man was when I was growing up? Where was he when I needed the love and attention of my daddy? I do not think that my disappointment ever went away. It was always there just beneath the surface waiting to erupt. That explosion would come later when my daddy moved to Georgia. He made the decision to take the car that I was driving (and had paid to have fixed, mind you) so that a lady he had met there could have transportation. I do not think it was really about a car but another occurrence of him putting these other people's needs ahead of mine, his daughter. At this point I was no longer interested in concealing or controlling the hate bubbling to the surface. It was obvious that he did not care about me, so why should I care about him? I cut ties with my daddy thus entering my fatherless days.

I went on to get married after getting permission from my mother. My girls and I moved from Columbia, South Carolina to Lusby, Maryland. I have no idea which one of my sisters filled in the blanks of my life for my dad. I really did not care. We were no longer sharing the same space. If he were at family events, then I did not attend. Although this would be disappointing to my family members, little did they know that it was for the best. I did not trust myself to be mature enough to dwell in the same space and not ruin whatever the occasion was even if they were momentous ones. Sure, I regret it now, but unfortunately that is the reality of where I was then. My self-imposed excommunication did not stop my daddy from sending cards for the holidays. During those years he kept sending cards with checks enclosed, just as he did with my siblings. He kept sending them even after I returned them. I was still his child even if I was not acting like I was. Just as we are still God's children despite our behavior. His hand is still extended. God gives us countless opportunities to accept His gift of unconditional love. Now, I can admit it probably wasn't the best decision I ever made, especially since the money would have helped, but it was the principle of the matter coupled with my position that I was done with him. I wanted to get the point across that I no longer wanted anything from this man…. not even his money.

Even when my dad's health began to take a turn, I was standing my ground. He needed a kidney transplant. The call went out for his children to be tested as possible kidney donors. I do not know what they did, I knew that I was not getting tested. I never entertained the thought of being tested. They needed to call those other kids he was so busy taking care of, not me. Call those non-biological kids that were long gone from his life and probably nowhere to be found. I stood firm on this decision because I believed that people reap what they sow. I felt that it was my job to make sure that this was the case for him. I mistakenly thought that God needed my help here. The truth is I was trying to make sure he hurt just as much as I had been hurt according to my view of the situation. I can see how this was not the Christianly behavior I preached, however I felt that my pain had no religion, only a deep-seated need for some form of revenge. After all, I had valid reasons for my behavior. I had a right to feel and act like that. I had mastered the art of justification. If he had not, then I would not have. Of course, on some level I knew this was the wrong attitude to have, and the wrong path to take. I would stand under prayers of forgiveness and release every Father's Day only to walk away with the same hatred and bitterness in my heart.

There came a point when I stopped being in those prayer lines. My feelings were not changing. The truth is, I did not want them to change. Some part of me did not want to trust God with my heart. After all, why should I be the one to forgive? Mark 11:24-27 explains it this way, "Therefore, I say unto you, what things so ever ye desire, when ye pray, believe that ye receive them, and ye shall have them. And when ye stand praying, forgive, if ye have ought against any: that your Father also which is in heaven forgive your trespasses. But if ye do not forgive, neither will your Father which is in heaven forgive your trespasses." Not to mention that the word "forgive" appears in the Bible over a hundred times. All this time my sins were going unforgiven by God and my prayer requests were being unanswered. But who was thinking about that when I was so busy being right?! I was waiting for God to realize that I was right to feel this way. Often, I wondered why a God who loves me would give me a daddy that did not? Where was my dad that the movies and television shows portrayed, or the dad described in those greeting cards that filled the shelves on Father's Day? Didn't I deserve that kind of daddy? But God, in His infinite wisdom gives us what we need, not necessarily what we want. For He knows what is best for us, even when we do not. Jeremiah 29:11 states, "For I know the plans I have for you, declares the LORD, plans to prosper you and not harm you, plans to give you hope and a future." I had no idea that there was such a plan or that it would save my life.

As his health began to diminish, I heeded the advice of my siblings and made the obligatory hospital visits in Georgia. Although I was present in body, I was absent in emotion and compassion. After a while, these visits only left me feeling pity for this man who had let his selfishness separate himself from relationship. I cannot even count the number of times I allowed my flesh to separate me from the things of God. Oh, how good it is to know that nothing can separate us from the love of Christ. All these years I considered myself a Christian even though I was not practicing a Christian lifestyle or acting like I had a Christian heart. It was still there buried under all my anger, hurt and disappointment. I had not trusted God with it. That became my prayer, but it was not an easy prayer to pray. Every time I thought that things were getting better, the enemy was right there to remind me of all the reasons why I should not forgive my dad. There were setbacks along the way as I rehashed the past, but with God's help, I was able to pull down the strongholds in my mind. Little by little I began to remember those good times that had been overshadowed by the bad. The enemy had stolen those memories so that I could only recount the bad. God will give you back everything the devil stole when you trust in His will for your life.

Time passed before my dad would make his last visit to Maryland. My uncle asked if he could bring him over to visit. I surprised us all by saying, "Yes." It was proving time for me. Time to put in action what I kept telling myself and everyone else: "I'm over it." So, I opened my front door and invited my dad and his new wife inside. The visit, although awkward at times, went without incident. A lunch was planned for the family and of course my uncle included me. I was shocked when his wife questioned my inclusion. Since it was for my family also, I made the decision to remain and focus my attention on everyone except her. I did not expect her to cry and be so hysteric from me ignoring her. At this point I was done! I drove my happy self to the hotel to tell my dad that I would not be a participant in the foolishness of her antics. I was good right where I was. This opened the door for us to have honest and open communication face-to-face.

This would be the conversation that would shed light on our fractured relationship. I was able to share with him my disappointment of not being a priority in his life. He shared with me that he had regrets about the way he had handled things, including the way he left our family. He admitted that he had made mistakes that he did not feel like he could correct. I would learn that I had once been a "daddy's girl" right down to him having to hold me as he cut the grass. I was reminded that out of all the kids I am the only one with a nickname, "Cheenie Bird." Do not ask, I have no idea where it came from. He shared that he saw the grandkids as his second chance. This conversation revealed things long forgotten and things I did not know. What meant the most was the apology. It could not change anything that had happened in the past, but it was a good start. Since I was well past the age of being fathered, we agreed to build a relationship based on civility with the hope of it developing into more. Small changes lead to big changes. You gotta start somewhere, and the change needs to be realistic.

I did not put much effort into forming a new relationship with my dad. I answered a few calls on holidays, and we exchanged some cards, and that was probably the extent of our relationship. It was not until I attended Bible study at the newly established Remnant of Hope International Church that I had a change of heart. The first series was about LOVE! Piece of cake, right? It was, until we were tasked with performing five random acts of kindness with someone, we did not have the best relationship with. Well, that changed things a bit. My dad was the first person to come to my mind. As I pondered that, Pastor Gross looked my way and said, "Yeah, that person." Why would I need to perform random acts of kindness for my dad if everything was good between us? The more I thought about it, the more I realized that things were not good. I would not need to contemplate it if they were, nor would I be hesitant to complete the task. So, I picked my dad to be the lucky recipient of my acts of kindness. I got things started with a text message, typing it, deleting it, trying to put together a message that was the perfect mix of nonchalance and concern. I followed it up with a short note that I had written and included a lottery ticket. My phone call was made last. I really was determined to finally let go of the past. Even more determined not to allow the enemy to steal any more of my time. He had stolen enough already. I had been robbed and would not realize to what extent until much later.

There would be more random acts of kindness. More hospital visits to see my dad who was steadily declining in health. The call came in the early hours of the morning. We needed to get to Georgia if we wanted a chance to say goodbye. I was on vacation in Florida with my brother and his family at the time. There were calls back and forth between my oldest sister and us. We had gotten emergency calls before, but this one was different. My brother booked us a flight on the first plane leaving. This would be my last opportunity to see my daddy. I was unprepared for the machines that were keeping him in some semblance of life. I was unprepared to be in a room with people I was not familiar with. All the same, I held my daddy's hand and softly whispered in his ear, "Daddy, it's Nessa. I love you. Don't worry about anything, we're good. You can leave knowing that we are good. You're my daddy and I love you." My dad squeezed my hand, and I knew he had heard me. These would be the last words I would speak to my daddy. He transitioned on April 13, 2018, with me by his side. My brother would later gift me with a picture that he had taken of us in these last moments together.

I am grateful to have been afforded the opportunity to say goodbye. I am aware that not everyone gets a chance to know when a family member is leaving this life much less be a part of the sendoff. God allowed me this time and I must admit that it helped me in my healing process. I have often wondered how different my life would have been if my daddy had been around. Unfortunately, my dad was a self-professed atheist. Would he have raised us as a family of nonbelievers? My dad's absence is what led my mother to the church. It is what had us in church twice on Sundays, Tuesday, Thursday, and Friday nights each week. Before he died, my dad would make references to God, and he even owned a Bible. My prayer was that he would be saved. I cannot say for certain if he ever did. One of my biggest regrets is that I did not model God's love to my dad. In my selfishness of being a right fighter, I missed an opportunity to be a witness of God's goodness to my dad.

Today, I stand healed of that part of my past. So, while we may never know why God allows the things that HE does, we can rest assured that nothing HE does is without purpose. Every trial, every tribulation is meant to produce a good work in us. Mine was meant to teach me to trust and not doubt. His perfect plan was at work saving me from a life of unbelief; drawing me closer to my Heavenly Father; causing me to prosper and grow in the Word. I do not need to know or even understand the whys and why nots of my life. I just need to know that my FATHER in heaven loves me unconditionally. Everything I ever needed was already prepared and waiting for me to access it. This FATHER of mine is present day and night, day after day and that is enough for me. Now I can honestly say, "Daddy, you were part of God's plan all along."

The LORD hath appeared of old unto me, saying, "Yea, I have loved thee with an everlasting love: therefore, with lovingkindness have I drawn thee."–Jeremiah 31:3 KJV

Pastor Margo's Heap of Hope

Love and forgiveness: two actions everyone wants to receive but find difficult to give. We love quoting scriptures about how much Jesus loves us. We have written songs like, *Jesus is Love, Yes, Jesus Loves Me,* and *He Loves Me.* There are less songs and few scriptures quoted about loving your neighbor as yourself. Loving others is so critical to the Christian walk that Jesus shows that it is the way people are to know that you are a disciple (John 13:35). Jesus' words emphasize that disciples are not known by their special clothes, long titles, or even how great they preach. Disciples of Jesus should be known by their love. Most people love people who do right, but Jesus followers love even when people do wrong. It is our love for God and His forgiveness of our sinful nature that allows us to have compassion and forgive others. Would the person you hold in bondage to the wrong they have committed know that you are a disciple? Would they agree or disagree that your love precedes you? Hurt is real. Pain is real, but so is the love of Jesus Christ. In fact, it is His love that covers a multitude of sin (I Peter 4:8). Aren't you grateful it covers yours?

Vanessa Tyler-Gantt Bio

Vanessa Tyler-Gantt was born to Jeral and Francy Tyler in Columbia, South Carolina. She is the wife of Derrick Gantt, Sr., mother of VaLisa and

VaLaya Tyler, and the grandmother of KyLeigh, DerRon and Layla. Vanessa has been married for 15 years and enjoys spending time with her family and friends laughing and creating new memories. Vanessa is known for being firm, funny and fashionable. She serves at The Remnant of Hope International Church and currently lives in Lusby, Maryland.

Contact Me:

Web: https://bit.ly/vanessatylergantt

Optical Illusion

"I went through life like a robot walking in a fog."

by Janice Mitchell Scott

Optical Illusion

by Janice Mitchell Scott

Every tear you cry strengthens you. I am convinced of this fact. No, it is not scientific, but my life has proven such. Malachi 2:16 NLT was one of the first verses I heard when I came to church. "For I hate divorce!" says the Lord, the God of Israel. "To divorce your wife is to overwhelm her with cruelty," says the Lord of Heaven's Armies. "So, guard your heart; do not be unfaithful to your wife."

God hates divorce, that is true. However, no one I ever heard quote that scripture finished it. The part about being faithful to your wife or being cruel to her was never brought up in the conversation. If I had read it for myself maybe I would have given myself more grace. Divorce is not an issue that is talked about at church. God hates divorce, but He never intended for us to live in bondage. My question for myself concerning my former marriage was, "Did God put my marriage together or did I?" I was in a marriage that looked like a happy little family. It was an optical illusion. Simply put, it was not what it looked like. We looked the part coming to church on Sunday color coordinated with our kids always looking the part, too. It was a façade. When the truth came, there was a trail of tears that was tragic and heart-wrenching.

My story had an almost fairy-tale beginning with all the freshness and butterflies of a new love. I met my former spouse at church. We both attended the military church near our current duty stations. Our courtship was short and not very eventful. We had a beautiful military wedding with all the pomp and circumstance to include the horse drawn carriage. Never would I have thought this polished military man that would become my husband was going to push me to a place of heartbreak.

I was very taken aback when we got pregnant immediately after getting married. I was excited and overwhelmed all at the same time. He was happy because he had no children. I came into the marriage a divorcee with two kids. So, getting another divorce was not an option. Our lives appeared normal in every sense until the layers were peeled back. The layers of denial, deceit, and disappointment became my constant companions. It seemed shortly after I got pregnant with our child, he no longer had any interest in me intimately. My weight was always my go-to excuse to justify why he did not find me attractive or would not even touch me.

We had been married about seven months when I heard a voicemail message on our shared cell phone of a man describing my husbands' private parts. Hearing the male voice gave me a sickening, nervous feeling, and cemented me in the very spot I stood. This could not be happening to me. I did it right this time. I met and married a man that was a Christian and attended church. He could not be talking about *my* husband. When I regained my composure, I woke him up. He had a story, and I believed it.

The next day we changed the phone number on the phone. However, that did not change his behavior. This was the beginning of an eight-year life-changing ordeal of living with a husband that was attracted to men.

Three years into the marriage I learned to live with his not wanting to be intimate or not paying attention to me at all. There were no date nights or hand holding. He watched television and spent time on his laptop or the family computer. There were the gay chat rooms, pictures of men, and secret email addresses. There were lies, stories and coverups. He had no interest in me at all except to keep the image of the perfect family alive. It felt like I was living in a *Lifetime* movie, but no one came to rescue me.

I was not innocent in the situation I knew the truth, but I did not want to deal with another divorce, or the embarrassment attached to it. You see, we went to church every Sunday and Bible study every Wednesday. We were both regularly active in ministry. At times we would argue all the way to church or not talk to each other at all. Despite the arguing, when we walked in church the masks came on, and we were the perfect family.

I do not remember the day numbness and loneliness became my constant companion. It just happened. One moment I was a well of emotions and then the next moment I felt nothing, just pain. Now, I think this was a God-given defense mechanism. If I had tried to deal with the totality of heartbreak, disappointment, and shear pain that was in my life I probably would have had a nervous breakdown. God is so gracious and kept me in ways I could have never imagined.

My best friend was my constant support, though I know she did not understand why I stayed married. God knew I needed her. I remember saying to her, "A piece of man is better than no man." I see now that this was flawed thinking and fed into my own struggles with my own low self-esteem, self-worth, and self-value. So, for years I allowed myself to believe this was what I deserved for all the mistakes I had made in my life. I told myself my kids needed a father and I needed his financial support. I had realized I was staying in a relationship that could have killed me.

My entire existence was so heavy, at times it was like continuously wearing a layer of coats that were hiding the real story. I did a dangerous thing with the pain and disappointment; I internalized the entire situation. At times, if you talked to me, I minimized the pain and disappointment as if they were normal. When I finally went to counseling, I told the counselor that my husband left me for another man. She looked me straight in the eyes and said, "You are not a man. He left you for a man, but you are not a man." It took me years to rationalize that thought in my head. I blamed myself for not being woman enough, not being skinny enough, not being pretty, or just not being enough. So, I hid my pain by eating too much or spending money and getting into debt. Do not get me wrong, it was devastating! But I was in church, and God hates divorce. These are the words I would tell myself repeatedly. Now, I can see I was holding myself hostage in the relationship using one scripture. While all the time quoting scriptures like John 8:36 (NIV) "So if the Son sets you free, you will be free indeed." Those scriptures were all I could hold on to somedays through the last three years of my marriage.

Several years later I went to visit my family in North Carolina. I got a call from my husband asking for the alarm code to the house. You see, when I left the day before, I turned the alarm on, and he had forgotten the code. At that moment, I realized he had not gone home from work the day before. He had stayed out all night while I was in North Carolina. I knew where he was and what he was doing. Before this incident, he had gone out and come home without his wedding ring on, and he had started to be out of the house a lot. During this time, a co-worker called and told me it was supposed to snow in the Washington DC area. That was a perfect excuse for me to tell my family because they did not know anything was going on in my marriage. So, I thought. Years later I found out my children had told my mother what was going on in the house. I loaded the girls in the car and headed back home. The entire time I thought he would be home when I got there. I called and called but he did not answer my calls or respond to my texts. I could not sleep or eat, and it took all my energy to go to work Monday morning. My older daughter had to take care of my younger daughter because it took all my strength just to get out of bed. Depression set in fast. I could not understand why my husband had left me.

I remember staring out the bedroom window for what seemed like hours, waiting with a heavy heart for his car to appear on our street. It was the first snow of the year and there was an eerie quietness about that snow-filled night that escaped me. I was trapped in my own personal emotional dungeon, that felt like it was caving in on me. At that moment, there was no hope for my marriage or my emotional state. Then it was like I felt hands lifting me and putting me to bed. Though sleep seemed like such a difficult task, after a few minutes this sweet peace fell over me. I did not know the journey that was before, but I knew I was going to make it through this. Looking back now, I realized I was holding on to the peace and hope only God can give.

During his nine months out of our home, he lived with two different men that I am aware of. In the marriage I was the one that paid all the bills in the house. This gave me access to the cell phone bill. I printed off copies of the cell phone bill monthly and there would be pages and pages of phone numbers that he called or that were calls to him during the month. Sometimes I would call the numbers and men would answer or I would get voicemail with a man's voice. It was like a morbid monthly ritual that I tortured myself with.

I knew God was with me even if I did not see Him nor could I always feel Him. I cried almost every day that year. Tears just kept coming and I had become a joke to some people. They did not understand the magnitude of pain that I was feeling nor the fact that my heart was broken in a million little pieces. I hated everything that made me a woman. Most of the time I avoided mirrors so I could not see myself.

After the first couple of weeks, I realized I could not make it through this without God. I was so broken that I would listen to sermons and songs to fall asleep at night. I would quote Jeremiah 29:11 (NKJV) "For I know the thoughts that I think toward you, says the Lord, thoughts of peace and not of evil, to give you a future and a hope." I learned I had to hold on to my faith. It was God that was going to get me through this, not me. My strength was failing, but I had hope. Even through the darkness of the marriage I had hope and still believed in marriage. Through all of this, I still wanted my marriage. I prayed and petitioned God to bring my husband back home.

I cut myself off from my family and friends, except, my best friend, who was my constant voice of comfort. I called her almost daily in tears it was so hard to deal with the heaviness and my broken heart. My heart was so broken that at times my chest literally hurt. Though I was at church every time the door opened, I did not share my story. Who would understand? I had never heard of anyone else dealing with the issue I had. No one talked about issues like this at church or in our community. There was a level of embarrassment and shame that I was not willing to deal with. The church I attended at the time had multiple services. I attended them all and went to the altar. The altar was my safe space because no one knew my story or struggle. If he did show up at church during the time of our separation, I always saved him a seat so it would look like there was nothing wrong.

God is a keeper because he kept my children. I could not be a mother because all I could see was my husband leaving me for a man. The pain and agony I experienced was crippling at times. I cried going to work, at work and on my drive home from work. By the time I got home, all I could do was cry and crawl in bed. I was depressed and broken-hearted, but I kept holding on. I needed God more than ever. I started having anxiety attacks and had to call my best friend or someone else to talk me through the anxiety attacks. One night my best friend stayed on the phone with me until 3 a.m. just so I could hear another voice. My sister-friend saved my life that night because no one knew I wanted to die. The pain I was feeling was real and it never let up, but I needed it to stop. One day I almost walked in front of a bus, but I saw my daughter's face and I stepped back on the sidewalk. The depression had taken me over.

Nine months later, he moved back home. That was a prayer answered for him to come home. We never dealt with why he moved out or his sexuality, and I did not care because he came home to me. I just needed him back. I really wanted my marriage. Remember, I said, "A piece of man is better than no man." I really believed God honored my prayers and faithfulness by putting my marriage back together. This euphoria only lasted about thirty days. He was back to hiding the cell phone and spending all his time on the laptop. He was angry with me and the children all the time. Something in me started to change, I became bitter, angry, and resentful instead of numb. I did not want to fail again but I could not live this lie. I went through life like a robot walking in a fog.

I serve a God that is so gracious and loving that He never left me alone and He did not let me die going through the process. Three years later, I came home from a trip angry and very cold. I did not know what was wrong with me. I prayed and asked God to soften my heart towards my then husband. The next morning when I left for work, I told him I loved him, and I wanted our marriage to work. That day was like any other day except I learned ten minutes after I left home that morning, he had gotten online trying to hook up with a man. The knowledge of his behavior was not going cripple me again. I was done, it was no longer my job to protect him and carry his secrets. The weight of being married to him was too much for me. That was the first time in eight years I felt free. I did not care how I looked to other people because they did not know what I was living through. I did not care about finances or other benefits; I knew God would provide for me. All I had to do is trust God and cast my cares on Him.

When I got home, I must have looked different because he knew something was wrong with me. I told him I was done with the marriage. I was going on a trip in three weeks and when I came back, he needed to be gone. He cried and even tried to blame me for his actions over the years. I was not having it. There was a strength in me that I never knew I had. I trusted God with all my heart, and I believed He would free me from this marriage spiritually, financially, and emotionally. I did not care about finances or image; freedom was my goal. I just wanted to get off the emotional rollercoaster that I had been riding for years. I arranged for the children to go to my mother's house while I traveled for the week, and when I returned, he had moved out.

I was ending the illusion of what people saw and beginning to deal with the truth of the situation. I was willing to die for people's opinions before, but now I was free, and I did not care how I looked to anyone. After he moved out, I saw God give me beauty for all my ashes. During the time after the divorce I truly learned that my value and worth come from God. My own optical illusion kept me in the marriage. The warped view of myself made me feel like the dysfunctional marriage was what I deserved. The healing process helped me learn that marriage is a commitment between the husband, wife, and God. It was the love of God that allowed me to walk away from the bondage of low self-esteem and finally realize who I was in Him. All those nights when I prayed for myself, I promised God that I wanted to help people going through divorce. I never want anyone to feel alone and helpless like I did. Now I look back and wonder what I would tell myself or another woman in the same situation:

- I was the one with the distorted vision of myself and the marriage. I believed my value and worth came from having a man. It was so much deeper than settling for him and what he was willing to give me. The true commitment and love of a marriage were something he could not give me.

- This event made me face some hard realities about myself. Since I was a teenager, I always had a boyfriend or husband. I felt incomplete or less than when I did not have a man in my life. The love I had been searching for my entire life can only come from God.

- I had to deal with why I was attaching myself to emotionally unavailable men. He protected me, redeemed me, and saved me from myself. I spent most of my life looking for love in all the wrong places.

- I learned that God's grace and mercy will cover you until you have the strength and ability to handle the situation. Out of my greatest pain I learned my significance, my strength, and my beauty. It is crazy, but today I look at myself and I see a fighter. God allowed me to learn who He is and who He made me. While I did not have the strength to walk away from the marriage, God gave me grace and mercy while I stayed. He kept me mentally, emotionally, and physically while He strengthened and prepared me to leave the marriage.

- God's never-ending love allowed me to heal and forgive my former spouse. I have no aught against him. I prayed for him and prayed God's blessings over his life. I ain't mad. The marriage made me see my strength and God's power over my life. God has forgiven me repeatedly. The hardest person to forgive was myself. I allowed the continuous abuse of my heart and my being devalued in the relationship. It took some work, blood, sweat, and tears. I did not always look good in front of people, and I did not care how I looked. I just wanted to be free from the bondage that had kept me imprisoned for so long.

- The marriage did not break me, it made me stronger. I learned more about myself and about what a great God I serve. I survived with God by my side every step of the way providing light when I could not see. It was not about my former spouse it was about me coming through this situation better, stronger and learning lessons from the experience. This test gave me vision that I never had before. It all worked together for my good, the tears, my fears, the struggle, and the experience.

- There is no pain nor resentment now. There are times that I will catch myself smiling when I think about that period in my life. That time I never felt closer to God and I was totally dependent on Him for life. God saw me and He kept me despite my own dysfunction.

- My husband's sexuality did not define me—God defines me. His choices did not give me my value or worth. God's Word tells me I am fearfully and wonderfully made; I am worth more than rubies; I am of a royal priesthood. This was the jolt I needed to get my vision for my life and myself together.

1 Peter 5:10 told me I would have to suffer a while, but the hope of God restoring me kept me fighting when I felt like throwing in the towel. There were days I was so enthralled in the pain that death felt easier. There was a constant voice in my head telling me that I deserved my current plight. The enemy tried to get me to give up on myself, life, and God. But I refused to die in the pit of despair and kept believing in God's purpose for me even when I could not see any light in the darkness that was trying to engulf me. I can see clearly now the pain is gone. There is no more illusion.

Pastor Margo's Heap of Hope

Life does not always go as expected. We have our plans, goals, and dreams, but ultimately life happens to us all. No one, and I mean no one is immune to trials and tribulations. Everyone has their own cross to bear (Luke 14:27). Even in these times our hope should not waver. Romans 8:35 tells us that tribulation, distress, persecution, famine, nakedness, peril, and sword do not separate us from God's love. Going through life's trials should not make you feel less loved by our incredibly loving Father. Dealing with disappointment, rejection, and feelings of abandonment do not indicate a disconnect from God. His word says that NOTHING has the power to do that. The word of God tells us to, "count it all joy when ye fall into divers temptations," because we profit from them (James 1:2-3). They build patience, experience, and hope. Be encouraged! It does not matter what life throws at you or how bumpy the road gets, God is our refuge, strength, and a very present help in times of trouble (Psalm 46:1). He will redeem you and deliver you. Wait on Him!

Janice Mitchell Scott Bio

Janice Mitchell-Scott was born in Kennedy, Alabama. She is the oldest of six children born to Bishop Levert and Linda Mitchell. She describes herself as a true southern girl. Janice has worked in the federal government for over thirty years. Twelve of those years she served in the United States Army, as a Communications Specialist. She has a bachelor's degree from Park University in Social Psychology.

Janice is married to the love of her life, Francis Scott. They have a blended family with seven children and five grandchildren. They live in

Accokeek, Maryland. The Remnant of Hope International Church led by Pastor Margo Gross is their church home.

Contact Me:

Web: https://bit.ly/janicemitchellscott

The Old and the New Life

"God had a different plan for me."

by Elder Michael A. Gibson

The Old and the New

by Elder Michael A. Gibson

I remember when I was a little boy growing up in the South, in Monroe, Farmerville and D'Arbonne Louisiana. D'Arbonne is spelled that way because of the French heritage of the southern part of the state. I went to an all-black school from 1967 to 1973, and in 1974 the Union Parish school system was desegregated, and all races went to school together. It was hard the first year because the white children looked down on us black children as if we were beneath them. Frank Morgan, my white counterpart, and I fought every day and I would always win. One day I asked him why he always picked a fight with me and his response was, "You were the biggest black guy in physical education class, and if I could beat you all of you would follow us and we, the whites would be the leaders. He was taught at home to hate black people but after he could not accomplish his feat of beating me, we became the best of friends and everything changed for the better.

It was great growing up in the country and living like *The Waltons*. Yes, there were that many of us. I grew up on a farm that had every kind of farm animal except goats. My job was to tend to the chickens and the pigs

70

which grew into big, big, big hogs. Life was simple. We did not have much growing up. We wore hand me down clothes which meant when the clothes got too small for the older children, they were not thrown away but passed down to the next child. It was easy to do because there were eight girls and five boys; five were stillborn which meant they did not survive. When my mom and dad would leave the house, they would leave one of the older kids in charge and us younger kids would be at their mercy. They thought they were mom and dad. We were and still are a large family.

My mom took us to church every Sunday. It was mandatory, and we could not slide out—no way no how. My mom would make me wear the same wool suit every Sunday with a necktie even in the summer months. If you know anything about the south, you know the heat would be unbearable at times. Our church back then did not have air conditioning. Instead, we had hand fans with a picture of Martin Luther King, Jr., and Malcolm X's faces on them. The preached word was powerful and true. Most times growing up in the South in the late 60's and 70's the word of God was all we had to hold onto. Prejudice was everywhere and there were places we could not go into. I experienced having separate bathrooms and being forced to go to the back of the restaurants to pick up our food when we ordered, despite the fact that it was all black people cooking and running the place. But that is how it was back then.

I did not like church because I was forced to go. It always seemed like all the grownups would run around the church when the choir sang, and the Pastor preached. I did not understand it then, but the Holy Ghost had fallen on them, and they could not be still. My mom told us it was a good thing and we should get it. I did not want it if it would make me act like they did, but little did I know that the Holy Ghost would fall on me when I was not even at church.

As I grew up, I left God and the church and lived my life wilding out. I eventually joined the Navy. I came home to visit my mother in Louisiana. She still lived in D'Arbonne Louisiana at that time and we were at the house. My mom had bought some land and had a Jim Walter mobile home put on the property. She lived in it even after my father had passed on. The house she and my father had built on the land they bought was just behind the mobile home. My mom did not want to live in the house any more after our father died, so that is when the mobile home came into the picture. It was good for her.

I was home from California visiting, and I remember this as if it were yesterday. I had come in from hanging out with my family, partying, and I remember my mom got up and let me in and yes, I was a little toasty (drunk and high), and my mother knew because I could not hide anything from her. Mothers often know just by looking at their children what they are up to. My mother knew because she did the same thing when she was a young woman growing up. But let me go back to the story about the Holy Ghost and how I came to experience him.

No, I was not in church. I had been partying, drinking, and doing whatever I wanted. Yes, you can only imagine. I spoke with my mom for a little bit and we went to bed. Mom went to the bedroom on the far end of the mobile home, and I went to the front bedroom. I was in a deep drunkard sleep, and I was tossing and turning but it really felt like the bed, and the room were spinning because I drank and smoked too much. I was going through a lot, and I could not get up no matter how hard I tried. Now, I know it was God who made me stay there in my mess. My head hurt so bad, my stomach was in knots, and I could hardly breath. I could not do anything to help myself. Sometime after the pain started to subside, I thought it was going to be over, but God had a different plan. My breath got short, and I tried to scream for my mother, but my mouth would not move. I started to cry while my mother was just a few steps away, but I could not call out to her. God had a different plan for me. I know this now, but back then I did not have a clue. I thought I was dying, and when I could do nothing God stepped in. and He started to shake my body, my feet started shaking, and then the feeling came up from my feet to my legs, and I was not in control. All I could do was let God have his way.

On June 10, 2000, in my mother's house, God saved me from myself, but it was nothing I did. My mother told me later that she heard everything that was going on and she went to her prayer closet and began to pray for me. See, I did not understand it then, but I do now. I am so grateful for my mother because that night she prayed for me when I was in my stupor and my mess, and God heard her and he heard me, but it was the prayer of a righteous woman praying for a wayward son who did not deserve to be here, but God. My legs began to shake and my whole body started to move; God sat me up in that bed and He turned my body to put my feet on the floor; His Spirit fell on me, and I started shouting and dancing in the house in the room. As God's Spirit filled me, I was praising God uncontrollably! I was giving God praise! I opened the bedroom door and started down the hall still praising God, mind you.

I went down to my mother's room to show her what was happening to me, but little did I know she was already halfway up the hall. Her posture was one of prayer. She just said, "I know." This was my first real Holy Ghost-filled and tongue-talking experience. The great thing about my experience was that it happened when I was at home with my mother and just me. So, when God says that when two or more are gathered in His name that He is in the midst, it is true. God is Lord, and God does what He says. We can just ask and believe according to Philippians 4:13 NKJV, "I can do all things through Christ who strengthens me."

I look back on that time and I thank God for saving me. I thank God for a praying mother who still to this day prays for her children. Three of us have transitioned on with the Lord, but there are still 10 of us that our dear mother, Inece Haulcy Gibson, prays for. She is a blessed and wise woman of 93 years young still going strong. She often says like the song, that she "feels no ways tired" and will keep running for God. God is good all the time and all the time God is good. I can write about this forever and ever. I can tell you of all the wonderful truths of God and how He has watched over me and kept me from hurt, harm, and danger over the years of my life.

While I was stationed in San Diego in the Navy, one Friday evening we were having a house party over some friends' house. The party was kind of slow, so me and two other people got into my friend's car and headed downtown to check out the nightlife for an hour or so. My friend drank a beer while at the party, so when he was driving and we were coming to a red light, he drove over the line a little and had to back up. I did not think much of it, but when we came to the next red light and the same thing happened, I was a little worried. We got through the lights and headed for the freeway. To get on this freeway there was a curve to maneuver through, and my friend started into the curve okay, but suddenly, his car sped up, and he lost control. He jerked the steering wheel back the other way causing the car, a Ford Van, to swerve to the right side. In doing so, the right rear tire on the van blew out, he lost control and the van started to roll. The van rolled over five times. How do I know you ask? I did not notice he wasn't wearing his seat belt either, and as the van rolled my friend landed on my chest five times and our friend in the back of the van wrestled with a small refrigerator tumbling through each of the rolls. Finally, when we came to a stop, the middle of the van was smashed down, and the doors of the van could not be opened! Our friend had to crawl out the back and my friend who was driving his van had to kick out the front windshield to get out of the van. Through every roll I was calling Jesus' name! We were all ok, just a little sore from tumbling. What I did not know was that my friend, the driver, had already drunk three mixed drinks before I arrived at the house party. He told me this after the accident. I know God brought me and my friends through that accident because we should have been dead. God used my body to save my friend because he was not wearing his seat belt. God watched over me and my friends that night and God is still watching over me and covering me.

I know God did it because He saved me, bought me, and shielded me from myself and from the rigors of this world. I try my best to live holy and acceptable to God, but I do not always live up to His standards. I am not worthy of God's love, and He shows mercy on me and lets me know that I am His child. He is my Father. He has a mansion with many rooms and there is one with my name on it. I am worth fighting for. I shout to the Lord all the time, and like my mother, I am no ways tired and I am going to run on for God until I cannot. I am so glad that I still have my mother, and I let her know. We all let her know that we, her children, love her and we give her flowers now while she lives. God is good and my life would be nothing without Him in it.

I have a beautiful wife, Patricia, and I have five awesome children: Dominique, Breanna, Daniel, Darrius, and Deshon; and five awesome grandsons. God is great and greatly to be praised. I pray my testimony will be an inspiration for those who read it to know that God is the great I Am. My dad, Warren Tom Gibson, is in heaven now looking down on us and seeing all the offspring that have come from him and mom. My siblings in order of birth are: Jessie May Gibson Mayfield, Helen Ruth Gibson (deceased), Ethel Bee Gibson Nation (deceased); Howard Gibson, Elaine Gibson, Larry Gibson, Evelyn Gibson Davis Simpson (deceased), Debra Gibson Westbrook, Blondie Gibson Webb, me, Claude Gibson, James Franklin Gibson and lastly, Debbie Maran Gibson. Yes, there are a lot of siblings, but we had the greatest and most fun times growing up. Dad and Mom raised us the best they knew how with what they had and what they knew. My dad finished school and went to the Army, did his time, got out and started a wood hauling business that was prosperous. My mom dropped out of school to be a mother but at 66 years old she went back to school and got her high school diploma. Amen! God is good all the time.

Pastor Margo's Heap of Hope

God makes all things new (Isaiah 43:19). He can refashion, repurpose, restore, and repair people for His glory. Simply put, Jesus changes people. Looking at Jesus' time on earth it is clear that no one met Jesus and stayed the same.

- The woman with the issue of blood bled no more (Matthew 9:20-22)

- The nobleman's son was cured and lived without ever meeting Jesus because His father did (John 4:46-54)

- Simon, James, and John caught more fish than they ever had and switched occupations (Luke 5:6-10)

- The man with leprosy was touched by Jesus (when considered "untouchable") and his body was restored (Matthew 8:3)

- The adulterous woman was rescued from a public stoning and forgiven (John 8:1-30)

We could go on and on about the mighty acts of God, not just in the Bible, but today. He is still changing lives one encounter at a time. He is still making ways, changing hearts, and cleansing us from all unrighteousness (I John 1:9). When we give our lives to Jesus, He allows us to live a glorious new life with Him. A life with purpose and meaning. His spirit gives us the power to change and choose the path of righteousness. Get in His presence and let Him change you, over and over again!

Elder Michael A. Gibson Bio

Michael A Gibson is an Avionics Technician III Lead at DynCorp International. He tests and evaluates software for the H1, H57, V22 Osprey, H60, and the H53 helicopters as a military contractor. Michael started his aviation career in the military where he learned his craft as an Aviation Electronics Technician. Michael tests and evaluates all electrical and electronic systems on these aircrafts. Michael also works with foreign

The Old and the New Life by Elder Michael A. Gibson

government allies to help develop their test teams with similar aircrafts. Michael is from Monroe, Louisiana, a dog lover, and a fan of all sports.

Contact Me:

You can email Michael at: michael.a.gibson@navy.mil or on his personal email at gibbyl2003@yahoo.com

Web: https://bit.ly/michael-gibson

God Kept Me: Gaining Self Love

"What you feed your mind, body, and soul is what you prosper."

by Nattasha Mackall

God Kept Me: Gaining Self Love
by Nattasha Mackall

I never would have thought that where God has me and where He is taking me in the year 2020 would have me feeling so free. So many curses, traumatic experiences, and life lessons could have taken me out. But God, He kept me.

When I was growing up people teased me about my thin figure, big bright eyes, or my long hair I usually wore in ponytails. I never thought this would be one of the first curses I would experience having, but I usually attracted the wrong people with unwanted advances to my personal space. I often had to deal with being bullied and teased because of my hair. Children amongst my race called me, "the cute, black girl with the long ponytails," and they treated me differently. Little did I know that this little girl would grow up and still be subjected to other peoples' torment because of their insecurities or lack of accolades. Whatever the reason, God kept me through the unwanted advances, the bullying, the ridicule, and opinions of others. Despite these things, later, you will see how God provided me with a son, whose gender was not even revealed until he entered this earth. I believe God sent me a son so that I could raise him to be a man of God who would not enter unwanted places, not make unwanted advances, nor invade other people's spaces. Glory!! My son would not be a statistic as a predator. God allowed me to bring a young boy into this world that will never be the aggressor like some of the aggressors his mom had to endure!

Moving on into my teenage years, I always wanted to attend the University of North Carolina (UNC) Tarheels but was unable to because of funding. I did not get a full scholarship, and quite honestly, things weren't set up for me to attend college. My counselor was honest with me and said he thought I had not put my best effort into my SAT testing. I agreed. I thought the test would be just like a high school test. I had always maintained a high GPA, so I thought I would take it, pass it, and be on my way. What a wake-up call. It was now time to find a job and somewhere locally to attend.

I regretted not having a college campus life. But God allowed me to get a scholarship from my high school, so I applied that and attended a business school. I held down both full and part-time jobs, and later attended community college. It felt good knowing that I worked for that and God kept me through it all; the long days, late nights, my travels to and from work and school, and the robberies that always occurred on my days off or right after I would leave. Later, I was able to get a job with the federal government and purchase my first home at 25 years old. Won't He do it?! It was not easy in the beginning, and I fell upon hard times a couple months and relied on people during the storm. I am thankful for them, but dependency was never what God had for me. He said for me to be obedient and use my own resources wisely and He would enlarge my riches, and He did what He promised.

Trust me when I say, when you become an adult people go all in on your life. I saw people change whether it was due to their lives or through them judging mine. One of my traits, love, is a blessing and a curse. I had to learn late in life that people loving you and liking you are two different things. They care about you enough to be there for you or envy you to the point where they would not be there for you. It touched me to my soul, not heart, but soul because some of these ways came from people that I would have expected to be there for me, not people that would say it's none of their business, or who would wait for me to say something. I thought about the ones listening and judging without the full story. There were those who got mad and upset over hearsay instead of reaching out to me for the truth during my separation and divorce, but God knows that they didn't get to hear my story because they didn't think it was their business. As I was suffering, I wasn't thinking of being the initiator in spreading my story. I was in pain. Presumed victims still have a growth process and if they don't attempt to mature, they will continue to create hostile situations. But I had to beware, victims like to play that they are the more reasonable ones. Stop expecting people to do what you are not currently doing yourself. Stop judging people for the decisions they make because you do not know everything. And, please stop thinking that though you have never been through something that someone else has been through, you may have a whole lot of answers to what their issues are but none for your own.

All this led me to wonder, God, where are You? Why are You letting people do this to me? You are all knowing. I said I can't take this, and God's Word hit me clear over the head; KJV Psalm 46:10 "Be still and know that I am God: I will be exalted among the heathen, I will be exalted in the earth." God knew my heart. My soul was not set up to handle the demise, betrayal, emotions, or all the long suffering. He told me it's not my fight, stand still, and He will handle them. So, guess what? When I had no one else, God kept me. I would often ask God, "Why me?" He would always answer, "Why not you? You have seen them do it to others. Why not You?"

People don't give negative energy to things that don't disturb their own spirits. God said there is something in me and while I break these chains there will be curses upon me. Praise be to God! He has done a lot of revealing. He revealed that people have a lot of internal demons. I chose not to take it personally any longer while reading a lot of healing books, it will state that people tend to remain victims. This gives them the attention that keeps them functioning without properly allowing themselves to heal. They want to internalize the hurt and pain as an excuse to behave recklessly. I realized that people act differently around other people when I was present because their conversation was different from when they were only around me.

The more I went back and forth with asking "Why me God?" the more I thought about a sermon I heard. One thing that stuck with me from the message is that growth happens where the seed is being watered. What you feed your mind, body, and soul is what you prosper. I learned that I had to get away from the narcissistic, controlling, manipulative, mentally and physically abusive people that I loved and was latched to because these people were only at a stage of like or tolerance. I was getting tired, I wanted God to convict them, because I knew they would not change on their own. God spoke again and took me to the verse, "Come unto me, all ye that labour and are heavy laden, and I will give you rest." (Matthew 11:28 KJV) I kept telling God it is weighing on me. I can't take it. My soul was shaken, and I got pulled to another verse, "I will lift up mine eyes unto the hills, from whence cometh my help. My help cometh from the Lord, which made heaven and earth." (Psalm 121:1-2 KJV) I was reading and fasting on these verses, still saying, "God get them! Get them! I can't take it." I was showing doubt. I wasn't standing still to hear or see Him working it out. I also did not see it because it wasn't resolved the way I wanted. God showed me either through those people or their surroundings, God does not want anyone to suffer, but I do know that He made some things happen to open some people's eyes. What I did not see, God saw, and those people will have to answer to God for what they said and did. God told me I am only where I am because I cannot see what He is trying to do. He had been working it out the whole time. My answered prayers will bring forth changes, but if I am praying for peace then I must receive what God will allow to remain or take away and He is peeling it all off. He has kept me. God continues to speak and show that peace will come with obedience and growth. Separation from turmoil does not make me better than others but it provides peace, and with peace comes obedience. It is not always easy but if I listen and adhere to what God says and stop letting man be a distraction, I will be a healthier me. Do not let people pull you into their storm. Sometimes, I regret not explaining my story, but I also know some people will believe what they want and have no intention of changing their minds. People cannot give me what they do not have. Some will be mad to know that yes, I am better, because I am choosing to be better. I did not fall. I was as low as I could get but God kept me.

As a mother, I had to get up and put on my crown and cape every day. Just because others saw the hustle did not mean the weight wasn't heavy. As a single parent, I find it hard when the burdens are heavy not to look like what I have gone through. I love like God does even when others seem undeserving. I do less reasoning why because most times it has nothing to

84

do with me. I realize it is true that hurt people hurt people. God will restore or remove the situations. By God's grace I break the many curses of abuse physically and mentally, finding peace and happiness in restoration of my soul and not people. I venture out more and speak less to be obedient and blessed. I realize I am going places that others cannot go. I may have to come back for them so that they do not disrupt the process. I have also learned to separate myself from people that continue to enable those that are destructive by learning self-love and creating a space that has boundaries. Many do not know my story because they stepped away during my storm. I have broken all chains. No person can fulfill me with the glory that my soul needs, but God. I have chosen to be obedient and I will turn a deaf ear to all the negative adjectives people describe of my life. To God Be the Glory!! And yet many of you do not console because you are bitter that in your time of mourning perhaps no one consoled you. God told me a long time ago to get up, he showed me the signs, but I stayed down too long. If only I had stood still to listen because, "The eyes of the Lord are in every place, beholding the evil and the good."(Proverbs 15:3 KJV) He sees what is behind and what is ahead, all the threats, all the dangers. "For God shall bring every work into judgment, with every secret thing, whether it be good or whether it be evil." (Ecclesiastes 12:13-14 KJV)

I was praying and He was showing, but I just did not want to believe. Why me? I have been down so low that all I had was God. He was the only way I was kept. That is what internalizing does. It drives you to the darkest place. But glory to God each day He sheds me from the storms, peeling back all the labels and I realize what I thought should be and what is to be true is what I need to lean on. Long gone are the days of "I thought", "I wish", or "I can." It is okay to know life will involve few and that peace comes before all others. It is good to understand that people's love can turn into like or tolerance without warning. It is their decision whether it is called for or not. God found fit to place my husband, John, in my life, my protector, my gentle giant, and I am forever thankful. We have history, but what has become of us now is greater than we expected. The story was ours, and it was judged decades ago. It was not always good, and some things were misunderstood, but through God, John's personal testimony and his challenges, God gave him a second chance at life. Thank you, J, for wanting and believing that God kept you for me.

This testimony is dedicated to my son, Christian. Please grow up and work smart and not hard. Be a man and handle your business. Be a curse breaker whether generational or in this forever-changing world. Seek God in your decisions and know there will be days you will feel God is all you have. Never feel you don't have a way out, but if you do, get on your knees, and pray in Jesus' name. Weep if you must, for He shed His blood for us; He knew these days would come. When you stand dry your tears of joy and know there were plenty of days, weeks, and years your mom endured the same. Remember not to give up or try and maneuver quicker than God. Trust me, it never works. Know that I will continue to encourage you to trust and obey God first and foremost knowing that He will always be there. "Be strong and of good courage; do not be afraid, nor be dismayed, for the Lord your God *is* with you wherever you go" (Joshua 1:9 NKJV).

Praise God, He kept me and showed me the way. He had to tap me out for me to get up, because I had been there too long. I was making it a residence. God is the strong tower, and He can make a way out of no way. He will do what He said He would do, in Jesus' name, Amen! The moral of my testimony is that God kept me through a lot of trying times. My trying times have not determined my destiny. I have learned to ask God for help and be still for the answer. I have learned doubt and fear do not pair with having faith. I am standing still and feeling the presence of God peeling it all off. I have apologized to God for staying too long. I have accepted that with self-love comes changes and possibly condemnation. God kept me long enough to see that it starts with Him and my obedience. I am learning that to love like Christ loves is the only love I am accountable for providing. In Jesus name, Amen!

Pastor Margo's Heap of Hope

The Lord is your keeper (Psalm 121:5). He preserves and protects His children. Through life's tragedies and people's evil plans, the Lord keeps us. He upholds us with His righteous right hand (Isaiah 41:10) and no one can snatch us out of the Father's hand (John 10:29). When you allow God to rule in and over your life, He becomes the foundation and stake in the ground that holds you up steady and sturdy amid life's storms. God is the ultimate security guard and sure defender. God's right hand stands for His strength and capabilities. He holds us with strength and capability. We are not standing because of our strength, but the strength of God. We may be unable to withstand all the threats and attacks alone, but we do not have to. We only need to stay in the Master's hand. Our desire should be to remain in the protective care of Jesus, whose strength is made perfect in our weakness (2 Corinthians 12:9). We can feel weakness, but we must also remember that in Him we live, move, and have our being (Acts 17:28). We do not have to carry the burdens of life alone. Our God keeps us. In fact, Isaiah 26:3 says that He will keep us in perfect peace if we keep our mind on Him and trust Him. Do not fret, God has you in his mighty capable hands. Rest assured!

Nattasha Mackall Bio

Nattasha V. Mackall, was born and raised in Calvert County, Maryland and lived most of her life in Chesapeake Beach, Maryland. She earned her diploma from the Calvert County Public School System before attending Fleet Business School and earning a certificate as a Legal Assistant. Nattasha began working for Prince George's County Correctional Center, and later attended the College of Southern Maryland earning credits towards a degree in Arts and Social Science: Psychology/Sociology. She has been an employee with the federal government for the past 22 years.

Nattasha loves to bowl, read, travel, and enjoy a nice oceanfront view. Her favorite seasons are spring and fall. She is a member of the Remnant of Hope International Church. Nattasha is newly married and has three children united through this union.

Contact Me:

Email: nattashamackall@gmail.com

Social Media - Facebook: Nattasha Mackall

Web: https://bit.ly/nattashamackall

Yet While I Was Broken Still I Rise

"And the words of my mother came to me to just believe in God and pray."

by John Mackall, Jr.

Yet While I Was Broken Still I Rise

by John Mackall, Jr.

My early life was nothing to brag about but because I had a praying mother, she made a lot happen. I grew up in poverty but somehow my mother always made sure we were fed, dressed, and attended church. I was the third oldest of six children. I saw a lot. When there was no way, my mother stopped and prayed. I saw when there was no food, warmth, or aid. All she had was God, her children, and a few special friends. She would always say, "No matter how people treat you, pray for them."

As a young child I was raised in an abusive household. Many nights I watched my so-called "father" beat my mother or force her to fix him something to eat once he arrived home late at night. Many times, I would ask her why she would put up with it. She would say, "Just pray. God will work it out." One night while sleeping in the car just to escape the smell of blood, alcohol, and the turmoil, she finally said enough was enough, and my mother found a way out for us.

When I entered high school, the choice was either work or play sports. Ultimately, I chose sports because when I was growing up chores came before everything. My mother said I could join those sports, but I had to find a way to get to them because she worked. I joined the football team and would have to walk home about five miles (which was about 45 minutes or so walking) whenever there was a practice or game. This was a sacrifice for wanting to use my talent and become a great football player. I knew after graduating I did not want to remain living in Calvert County, because there was just so much more, I wanted to venture out to do and see. I moved to Prince George's County and worked for a few construction and restoration companies. Later, I found that working for others was not my thing.

During my highest-level of working, my first tragedy occurred. I was on my way to work and a tanker truck made an illegal U-turn and at 45 miles per hour I plowed into it and was entrapped in my work pickup truck. I blacked out, woke up in a hospital bed covered in tar and glass, listening to the doctors say, "What are we going to do? We've seen nothing like this before." I was still wondering what exactly happened. Later, the police officer told me that I was very lucky because two more inches and I would have hit his gas tank. Everything on the back of the truck flew off except two 100-pound propane tanks which I had just filled. The doctors told me I may never walk again. My first thought was I did not survive poverty, household traumas, and feeling like I'm at the best place in my life to be told by the doctor my life would never be the same. With lots of therapy, determination, and my mother and family's prayers I was able to walk out of the hospital in two months like I told the doctors I would. When I was placed in the wheelchair headed to the lobby my mother looked at me and said this was nothing but God. They gave me crutches and I stood up and with the help of the crutches walked to the truck. All I could think of was they told me I was not supposed to be here, yet still I rise.

When I recovered, I became more determined because I knew I had my young son, John, III, to raise. I loved a challenge, so I ventured out with minimal savings and started my own roofing company. All was going well until I installed a roof on a residence and a fire started which caused extensive damage. About a year later while installing another roof it began to storm, but the crew and I could not get the roof covered in time which caused extensive water damage to the restaurant. While I wondered what else could go wrong, I also thought my business license might be jeopardized. I was out there working, getting into things, and just feeling like I was going to do me and just live life. That is exactly what I did with no regrets. I felt I could not lose anymore.

The second most devastating thing was the day I received a call and my sister Maxine said our mother was at the hospital and was unresponsive. I cannot tell you to this day—and that was almost 30 years ago—how I drove from one county to another. When I got to the hospital, I was told that she was gone. Everything in the hospital lobby seemed to fade, and all I could not believe that was my mother, the one that always held me down!! As we were in the lobby the receptionist came over and said someone was on the phone for a "John," but when I said, "Hello?" there was no response. The line wasn't dead. It was like someone was just listening to me saying, "Hello?" I want to believe that was her way of saying see you later because I had always told her that if she ever passed I would never want to see her that way, I would want to remember her smiling face.

At the time, I honestly believed life would never be the same. When I left the hospital, I knew the next dreadful thing would be to tell my son John that his grandmother/best friend had passed. When I told him, he said I didn't have to tell him this, he already knew. After the family laid her to rest, I really started thinking about how God just took the most important person from me; the one that called on Him daily, even in her worst. Even when others treated her and her children badly, she always prayed, so why her? To this day I still don't know why God took her only to have those that caused her so much pain to still move on. I can still hear her telling me don't feel that way just pray; maybe it's my time. God knows best.

In 1993, my life forever changed. It was my sister's wedding day and this beautiful young lady caught my eye. At the reception table I told my brother-in-law and my sister that this lady would be my wife. I could not take my eyes off her. One of my most life-changing events was leaving the reception early so that I could cut ties with everyone so that if she asked if I was available I would honestly be able to say yes. I figured if this worked out it would keep me striving and give me the much-needed break from all the tragedies I had endured. Well, it worked. Finally, after getting to know this young lady for about two months, we hit it off and made our relationship official. Life appeared to be back on track, and all was good until years later when some changes occurred. Like most relationships we had our ups and downs, break ups and make ups only to realize this was not going to be our time. Much later I started a relationship with someone else. During this time my beautiful daughter, Jon'esse aka "Baby Girl" was born, and my life was good again. Then came a third tragedy.

It was a bright sunny day, and I was relaxing at home. I received a call from my youngest brother, Kevin, with the news that our oldest brother, Gordon—who was my protector—had passed away in an unexplained automobile accident. The news took me straight to my knees! I said, "God, not this again! Not him." The reconstruction of the accident made no sense. It was almost unbelievable the way officers said it had happened. And the words of my mother came to me to just believe in God and pray.

Everything was going well and here came the fourth tragedy. One of my dearest friends and business associate, Impeng, passed away. He gave me a business contract to perform work for a multi-million-dollar condominium complex. I started off my business with just completing small projects, soon thereafter I became the primary contractor onsite. Sadly, after years of working together and being the best of friends, unknowingly Impeng abruptly passed after finishing a job. I recall the prior night sharing laughs and having some wine. When I returned the next morning to complete the project, I was told by his wife that he had either passed in his sleep overnight or early that morning they were not sure. The pain was devastating and once again I heard my mother's words to just pray and believe in God. I put Impeng's death to rest and moved on. Life seemed to be good.

In the year 2012, I was up late one night watching television and a commercial came on about cancer. The commercial posed ten questions. If you answered yes to at least five, it suggested to get checked for prostate cancer. I answered yes to all ten. It took about a month for me to get up the courage to set an appointment for a routine check. Finally, I scheduled a doctor's appointment, got tested and was diagnosed with Stage IV Prostate Cancer. The specialist said that I needed to address this at once due to my test results. Within one week, radiation treatment began. Here I was again facing another life-challenging situation. Right away I knew I was not going to accept this for what it was. If the tanker truck did not take me out neither was the cancer. I frowned upon the word cancer because I saw what it did to some people I had known. So, from that day forth I called it a challenge.

During my time experiencing my challenge four of my friends and my cousin Gerald, all passed away from this deadly disease. I told God not me because I shall rise. Radiation totally wiped me out. There was not much to do. I couldn't work since I was going from one appointment to the next and seeing one specialist after the next. I went from not taking a single aspirin to taking about 15 medications per day and injections every few months. Now I was at my lowest point. The only thing that kept me smiling and alive was that I had to live for my children. After finding out my numbers were low at my last treatment, I could somewhat function again but now as a cancer survivor.

The doctor said that stress was not an option, but how can I not stress? In addition to everything going on there were major changes to my life and household. I needed to rise, and I did! I have since reunited with that young lady from 1993. She is now my wife and her son, Christian, a.k.a. "The Boy" is a welcome addition to my children. With God first, my family, and friends as my strong support system I have no doubt that once again I am healed, and I am strong. God's not through with me yet. He is showing me my purpose along with His plan and showing me how to be still and know that He is God as I trust and believe.

"The LORD is my shepherd; I shall not want. He maketh me to lie down in green pastures: he leadeth me beside the still waters. He restoreth my soul: he leadeth me in the paths of righteousness for his name's sake. Yea, though I walk through the valley of the shadow of death, I will fear no evil: for thou art with me; thy rod and thy staff they comfort me. Thou preparest a table before me in the presence of mine enemies: thou anointest my head with oil; my cup runneth over. Surely goodness and mercy shall follow me all the days of my life: and I will dwell in the house of the LORD forever." (Psalm 23:2-6 KJV)

Even after all the brokenness I still rise!

Pastor Margo's Heap of Hope

If you have ever been broken, you know what it feels like to have the life you once knew scattered into pieces. Not the kind of broken that only requires a little finessing of a few pieces or a small amount of glue to restore—No, not that type of broken. I mean the type of brokenness that is beyond your ability to fix and you are out of solutions. The hurt you feel cripples your ability to see beyond the pain. It is in this brokenness that we must be reminded that God takes marred pieces, fractured souls, and what we may believe is irreparable, and irreversible and makes a masterpiece. Our evidence is found in Jeremiah 18:4 as we discover a potter doing a work on the wheel only to find that his work is broken, flawed. The potter does not discard the clay. The potter knows that you can take those same ingredients and create another vessel that is equally as good or better than the original work. Your broken life does not make you ineligible for use by the master. He simply takes what made you and makes it over. Maybe your life is broken beyond a mar.

Maybe you are having an Ezekiel experience where you are looking at a valley of dry bones. Maybe your brokenness feels like corpses and the remains of what was once living, but since has no evidence of life. Ezekiel 37:1-14 reminds us that even what has been broken unto death can be put back together, resurrected, and receive new life when God is at work. Give Him your ashes, give Him your mourning, and your heaviness. He will take your broken pieces and breathe into them beauty, joy, and praise. God specializes in the impossible. Every broken thing in your life can be put back together again. Even the bones shall live.

John Mackall, Jr. Bio

John Wesley Mackall, Jr. was born and raised in Calvert County, Maryland. He graduated from Calvert County Public Schools. After graduating and working for other companies, John determined that working for himself was his goal, so he became an entrepreneur and started a roofing business, Mackall Family Contracting, Inc. Later, he ended this business and worked as a superintendent for a waterproofing company. While working in this position John created another business, Mackall Family Services, where he is an expert in restoration and a contractor for a multi-million-dollar condominium complex.

In his spare time John loves to travel and venture out in the woods to hunt, do archery, and camp. The woods are his quiet place; however, being by the ocean is his peaceful place. John is a member of the Remnant of

Hope International Church where he and his family worship. He is newly married and has three children united through this union.

Contact Info.

Email: mack1jr@yahoo.com

Facebook: John W. Mackall, Jr.

Web: https://bit.ly/johnmackalljr

Blindsided

"Most days I realize that God is in control."

by Paris Brown

Blindsided by Paris Brown

If I did not tell you, you would never really know the grief my heart feels. And to be honest, for many years I have done my best work not to show my heart by keeping my feelings to myself; not talking about the grief and the way I feel. Why? Most days, it does not matter! Most days, my family needs my strength and my smile. Most days, I am too consumed with being so "strong" for everyone else around me at home, at work, and in my relationships, that there's little room to be weak. And most importantly, I usually realize most days that God is in control.

I say most days because up until recently, there have been more days than not, that I have questioned God. It may not seem like a big deal because we have all gone through a stage in life where what God is doing and why just doesn't make sense or seem to line up with His promises. This time was different for me. For the first time in all my life; all the scriptures I learned as a child; all the time spent in God's Word as an adult; all the ways God has shown me He is faithful and has never left my side, all quickly faded away as I found myself unprepared for one of the greatest fights of my life. This was not just the typical marital discord or issues with a rebellious child. This fight led me to the place of not only questioning God and struggling with believing God at His Word, but I sometimes wondered if He was even real as my heart tried to convince me that God had outright abandoned me. In fact, it was just a short time ago that I hated God. YES, hate is a strong word. Writing this down shocked me as well, but I would be lying to say it was not a real feeling just a few short months ago. So, to understand my honesty, you must take a walk in my shoes.

For the most part, my story isn't any different than most testimonies of women growing up in the 'hood where poverty is often coupled with a lot of dark days living in the low-income projects, and creates a desire to overcome. My parents were the epitome of change makers who worked hours on end to take care of us. They did everything in their power to ensure poverty never left us feeling poor! They poured into us in ways that transcended our social-economic status and ultimately gave us a glimpse at what life beyond California's Bay Area streets could be. Despite our environment, every day of my childhood my father told me I was the most beautiful girl in the world and my mother set the best example of a strong, graceful African American woman. The reality, however, was that life was emotionally tough for this little black girl, so I often used my dimpled smile to hide the real thoughts and insecurities going through my head.

I quickly realized being tough was the way to survive growing up exposed to violence, gangs, and drugs that were magnified and controlled the community. The streets quickly gave me an impression of what tough should be, but it was mainly through watching my older brother navigate between the streets and classroom that I realized he is probably the toughest person I know! He did life differently with a level of honor, integrity, loyalty, and respect the streets had not seen. Our closeness taught me how to fight physically and emotionally and use my past to empower others to rise above challenging circumstances. So yeah, I could confidently say, I came from a strong cloth. That is, until I was blindsided three years ago by a storm that tested just how strong I was. This test tried everything I thought I knew about myself and my God. Sadly enough, I never saw it coming!

Truth is, life was not perfect, and I struggled big time with the internal torment of not feeling good enough, pretty enough, or being dealt a fair deal in life. I learned as a child how to perfect the art of using a smile to mask how I really feel—that is until I was blindsided and forced to face those same fears and emotions I had worked so, so hard to bury. Problem is, I did not want to be "strong" anymore! Matter of fact, I did not know how to be strong anymore because I was too weak to be tough and my emotions were bursting at the seams; but this is exactly where God needed me. What got me here?

As I stared into the hospital mirror at 4:02 a.m. on May 2, 2017, I quickly realized this would not be a normal birthday. Waking up from the most uncomfortable two-hour sleep a hospital chair could provide, it was almost as if God snapped His fingers and life as I knew it drastically changed. While rushing home to get the kids ready for school, tears fell and for the first time, I admitted to myself that I was angry with God! It was only a short drive, but I cried and cried, yelling at God, and questioning how and why God could leave me like this. I felt He had lied to me for so long. What was that lie? That things would be okay. That I would make it. That this life we have built over the last 17 years wasn't coming to an end, and that God would honor that little girl from the projects who had dreams of one day making a difference. By the time I realized it, I had pulled into my driveway, plastered on that fake smile, and convinced my kids that daddy would be okay. We didn't have much time to talk nor could my heart answer too many questions, so I selfishly pushed them out the door to school, and off to work I went—never to really deal with the emotions of the situation again. Too many people needed me, and I had to hold it together, or so I had convinced myself. We would be good; but as my night ended back in that uncomfortable hospital chair, what didn't change was how angry I was with God.

For the next two years, it felt like Groundhog's Day! We were working on autopilot as our lives changed dramatically with my husband's Crohn's Disease diagnosis. What was once the two of us ripping, running and traveling all over the east coast watching our children live their best lives, turned into a solo mission as my husband, often suffering from the symptoms of the disease, simply could not get out of bed.

Early mornings eventually turned into late nights behind the wheel shuttling the kids from activity to activity, and as much as I would do anything for my kids and family, I slowly started to hate the life I lived. Quiet as kept, I became angry with God, with my husband, and life in general. A support system would have been great at this point, but support systems are only as great as you allow them to be. "How dare the 'fixer' ask for help," is what I often convinced myself of. I had grown so used to helping solve everyone else's problems and being the strong friend that my pride wouldn't allow me to ask for help. So, I often sucked it up but grew angrier. And then there were the times I obviously needed help yet felt like no one was around to talk to, to wipe my tears, or to simply see Paris in the process, and so I became resentful of my husband since the focus was often on his wellbeing.

As my husband grew more and more ill, I found myself often alone, almost living as a single parent in my head. It felt like my husband was never awake long enough to talk to about anything more than business. The best friend I once had in my husband had grown cold and often short, simply mean and hard to be around, so day after day and night after night, I bottled up my emotions and sucked it up just praying to get through one day at a time. On the inside I was suffering as it felt like life was choking me; yet on the surface, it appeared life was grand! Until one day I was faced with the inevitable question that I knew would one day come, but out of immaturity, avoided for some time— "What happens if daddy dies?" The question coming from my then five-year-old rocked my core!

Up until then I was used to that mask I wore daily. I was even almost okay with the exhaustion, sacrifices, loneliness, and the threat Crohns had become to my marriage; but never once had the thought of losing my husband crept into my mind. Maybe I was naïve. I left home at 18 and we have been together since we were only 19 years old, so my entire adult life was built around our relationship and family. I wasn't prepared for this conversation and as much as I tried to hide every single tear that fell as I drove that day and reassured my youngest one that, "Daddy will be okay. He would never leave us." The question sank into my heart and held it hostage for literally two years.

That two years felt like a complete lie! I not only lied to myself, but to my family, my friends, any, and everyone who simply wanted to know how I or we were doing. My husband became more and more ill and all I knew to do was to pour myself into church and our kids, so I never adequately addressed my emotions or fears until one day when driving over the Thomas Johnson bridge. As I got to the top of the bridge, I envisioned what it would be like getting out at its height and disappearing into the water below. Time had stopped and my mind became consumed with the thought of taking my own life just to quiet the thoughts that haunted me daily. A picture in my foyer of the three babies God had entrusted me with, broke my gaze and flooded my eyes with tears as I drove.

I never spoke about that day. There was no need to because although it did not change the fact that I was angry with life, it simply existed to show me my reason to live again. I had finally gotten to a place where I was able to admit the days where I was not okay and that THIS is what God meant when He designed marriage for better or worse. Those words never meant much to me prior to my husband's diagnosis because they had no reason to. Life was showing me otherwise and convinced me that though this was not the worst I would see in my life, God needed us to go through this for a reason. What that reason was, we had no clue, nor did we know that the test was not over.

Boog is the little girl I was terrified and excited to have all wrapped up in one. From the moment she spoke, I knew she was here for a reason and I fell in love with her instantly. She has always been a daddy's girl and loves her father much like I love mine. Her and my husband's bond has always been unbreakably special like a father-daughter relationship should be, so I often would watch their friendship and love with a smile. On the days he was his sickest, Boog would pay special attention to my husband's needs and at the slightest grimace or indication of pain, we would find her snuggled up next to him on the floor and fast asleep next to her protector. I think that is when I realized his illness wasn't just impacting me, but it had a huge effect on all of us.

When I struggled to keep it all together, Boog comforted me and became my strength. She would naturally become a nurturer and peacemaker, so our rides home from church or basketball were filled with discussions about God's faithfulness and plan in our lives as she was eager to keep my mind off our circumstances. I think that is what I adore most about her—that even in the face of desperation and uncertainty, Boog never wavered! In fact, Boog has embodied strength and faith like that of a seasoned saint as she too faced the fight of her life.

And that's where we found ourselves January 2020, as she and I made ourselves comfy in her private Children's Hospital room, awaiting results from a day of testing and concerning doctor's reports, eager for answers to why Boog had physically become someone we barely recognized. We had finally gotten to a place where our family could successfully navigate Crohns and worked to minimize the impact my husband's flareups would have, and then boom! Boog became ill. For months, she had fevers, lost her hair and eyebrows, and large amounts of weight; and slept most of the days away. We sought help from her pediatrician who randomly diagnosed Boog with multiple unrelated illnesses, but our hearts knew something greater was the underlying cause of her suffering. We spent hundreds of dollars and hours in local hospitals to no avail, so as you could imagine, the news of Boog's admittance into Children's Hospital was a huge relief yet caused a host of fears and worry to set in.

I admitted to Boog that I was worried yet trusted God with her life. As Boog held my hand, she assured me that even if her okay was not what it was before, she would be okay. It was in that moment that though I realized I was not prepared for yet another test, my tears shifted from sadness to admiration of the woman God was birthing Boog to be. It was hard to believe that my 14-year-old baby knew the severity of what this hospital stay meant yet was so firm in faith and so sure of God's plan for her life.

As we remained in the same hospital room for days, I watched Boog praise her way through the tough times. The times I would return from the hospital cafeteria to her listening to worship music or the times she would ask clarifying questions about God's Word, showed me that she knew the Lupus diagnosis is less about her and only about God's glory. But it was the times I watched her cry out in pain, so overwhelmed by the process and treatments, that I realized I needed to be strong for Boog and not the other way around like she had so often been for me. This time was different though. As much as I questioned God and was heartbroken watching Boog lose the beautiful curls I adored or suffer in silence from such a devastating disease, my questions were less, "Why me?" and more, "Why her?"

It could not be possible that I could potentially lose her also! My heart refused to believe that God would take both my husband and Boog away from me, yet I finally had to ask myself so what if He does?! And that was the moment God brought me to my knees and on my face, finally admitting that I couldn't do this alone and needed every ounce of Him to be everything Boog, my husband, my boys, and I needed when we needed Him most. Was this the moment He was waiting for all along? Why did it take me so long?

I remember sitting in the parking lot at work crying out to God, begging for His compassion and mercy, just needing Him to step in and be the God I remembered Him to be and just like that, He answered me.

He has always been those things. He just needed Paris to step out of the way so He could show me. God's Word says that, "[the] name of the Lord is a fortified tower; the righteous run to it and are safe." (Proverbs 18:10 NIV) He was waiting for me to run to Him as my place of refuge and my safe place!

From that moment on, God showed me just what that meant as we were overwhelmed with a church family and Pastor that prayed with and for us. They blessed and loved us so unconditionally that it challenged yet mended every ounce of brokenness our family had previously experienced due to church hurt. To make it even better, God sent angels in the form of friends that I am forever grateful for. Now don't get me wrong, there have been too many friends to count who have called, texted, held my hand and stood by, made sure I ate and offered to help with the kids during this season, so this is not to diminish anyone else's love or forget how others got me through; I simply realize that God needed me to experience friendship in a new way so that I could see Him more clearly, and He chose them to do so.

On those days I needed someone to be a friend who could help me forget about my circumstances, refocus me on my strength and wanted nothing in return but to help me smile, Asiah was the sigh of relief and sister God knew I needed. On those days I simply wanted to give up and felt the world crashing down on me, I'd get a text from Janice or an unexpected sign of her love, that gave me hope and most importantly, showed me what unconditional love is like. On the days where questions of God's love were constant and I needed to admit to someone I was scared, He sent me LaKesha to flood me with God's promises and cheer me on even when I didn't believe in myself. On the days I needed a reminder of who I was and who God was creating me to be through this test, God would send Patrice to remind me of His Word. Even through tears, she would find a way to make me laugh a good laugh and refocused me on the beauty of the 21 years my husband and I have shared together. She would never sugarcoat the tough times and held me accountable yet loved me and gave me room to admit that it was rough. On those days I'd walk into work, eyes bloodshot from crying and heart completely broken, it was Wendy who spoke life and encouragement over me and my family, and always gave me the hug my heart needed in those moments. And then there was my mom. I have always loved her and knew that as much as we bump heads, my mom would travel the world and sacrifice everything to ensure her "Petey" was okay. During the most trying time of my life, this was no different, as my mom became my friend. I could vent to her in a way I couldn't anyone else, she never told me my feelings were wrong or out of sorts, and always assured me it would be okay even from 3,000 miles away.

For a while, I looked in the mirror and asked, "Why me?" And finally, it hit me, "Why not me?!" I wanted to let go so many times. I even remember praying an honest prayer hoping I would never wake up again. So many times, I just needed God to take Crohn's and now Lupus away and to in a blink of an eye, make everything okay. So many times, I cried myself to sleep asking God why me, but as much as I fight saying this, I was handpicked by God for this life, and He knew what it would birth if I could just hold onto His hand. What was not clear in the storm, but I realize now, is that I wasn't necessarily blindsided by the test, but I was blindsided by God's grace and mercy. I thought Crohn's and Lupus would break me or better yet kill me. I thought that I could do it on my own and did not need anyone, let alone God to get through. I thought that being strong meant being the David Copperfield illusionist of emotions in public despite suffering silently and internally. I thought that there was no way out, BUT God showed me He is greater! His grace and mercy kept me. His grace and mercy surrounded me on even the toughest days, and His grace and mercy walked me through the tunnel so that I could see the light more clearly. I see God now and He has my undivided attention— my complete and undivided attention!

And so now I am able to focus on what is important in life like enjoying the day Jelani stuffed himself with donuts after not being able to eat them for years; or the days he and I just sit and talk, laugh, or debate sports as best friends; or the morning Boog walked out of the house with the most beautiful smile and in a new head wrap she was gifted despite losing almost 55% of her hair now; or the announcement of her getting the lead role of Carmen Diaz in the middle school musical "Fame"— a role she auditioned for after missing a week of school, multiple visits to the hospital and suffering silently with lupus, yet we had no clue; or seeing my oldest son's name in the local newspaper, honored for making the Honor Roll and defeating the odds during what I know has been a test of his faith as well; or reading a letter my youngest wrote to his sister admiring her for her strength and assuring her he loves her; or sitting at both my boys' basketball games, losing my mind in the stands from excitement of watching them stand tall in the face of what our family is going through and excel at something they love; or the times the kids and I drive to school and stand in awe of some of the most breathtaking sunrises God's hands can create.

This Job experience has helped me to cherish the small things and to show my family just how much I count it a blessing that I can call them mine! Would I be able to say these same things had we not gone through the last three years, I can't say that; but what I do know is that God is bringing us beauty for our ashes. God did not intend to break me; He needs to use me, and like Isaiah said, "Here am I, Send me" (Isaiah 6:8 NIV)!

Pastor Margo's Heap of Hope

Life can shift suddenly. Our routines and patterns make it easy to take the mundane for granted. It is easy to undervalue wellness, provision, and peace until they are disrupted. Have you ever had the tides of life come rolling in without warning or preparation? Have you experienced a whirlwind of unexpected change that you felt ill-equipped to handle? It happens to the best of us. We are minding our business and boom, the unexpected shakes us at our core and challenges everything we thought we knew. David writes that he would have fainted unless he believed to see the goodness of the Lord in the land of the living (Psalm 27:13). David makes it clear that unless we hold on to our belief that good can come from the most unexpected and tragic events we will faint. Our belief is the assurance we hold fast to when there is nothing left to grip.

We have this hope; while life can shift suddenly, our God can move quicker. He has a resume full of suddenlies. Acts 2:2 confirms that God's people of various nationalities were gathered on the day of Pentecost to do what they planned to do. They were interrupted by a sudden sound of a mighty rushing wind that filled the house. They were filled with the Holy

Ghost and began to speak with other tongues. It was not expected. They had not prayed for it. They were minding their business when God suddenly showed up unexpectedly and blessed them beyond measure. Know this, life can shift suddenly, but God does it better. He's sent a counter suddenly, that sweeps through your life and blows your mind. "For I reckon that the sufferings of this present time are not worthy to be compared with the glory which shall be revealed in us" (Romans 8:18 KJV). What God has for you is so much greater than your suddenly it is not worthy of being spoken about in the same sentence. He will do great things for you, suddenly.

Paris Brown Bio

Paris Brown was born to parents Dwight and Kimbely Barnett in 1980. As a California native growing up in the Bay Area projects, Paris realized the power in advocating for the rights of others and, while being a lawyer was her goal when she moved to the East Coast to work in large non-profit corporations, her eagerness to serve eventually settled her in the educational system of Calvert County Public Schools. Currently Paris is an Educational Liaison for Prince George's County foster youth. As a scholar, she graduated in 3.5 years Cum Laude with a Bachelor of Arts in Political Science from Morgan State University where she became a member of Sigma Gamma Rho Sorority, Inc. and this year celebrates 20 years as a Sigma Woman. Upon graduation, Paris obtained a Master of Arts in Philosophy and Social Policy from American University, where she tackled complex social issues as an intern for the Maryland General Assembly. This experience grew Paris into a passionate advocate for education, special needs youth, and those often marginalized, as evident in her various post studies testimony before the Maryland General Assembly on issues involving a living wage for educators and educational support staff rights across the state.

Her family can attest that Paris has been writing all her life. Whether it was helping her older brother with his papers and job applications, developing resumes and business plans for family members, or creating greeting cards for every occasion as a child stamped with her self-created logo "Dad's Favorite Girl's Card Shop," writing is what Paris does very well. Out of that love for writing, Paris launched, "The Write Vision by Paris" in late 2018 to formally help take others to new places through her writing. Her business is modeled after the belief that with the right resume and business plan, the world is yours!

Paris lives in Southern Maryland where she is devoted to Jelani, her husband of sixteen years, and their three children: Kimani, Caelyn and Keran. They eagerly serve and worship at Remnant of Hope International Church, under the leadership of esteemed Pastor Margo M. Gross. In her spare time, Paris can be found making her great grandma's peach cobbler recipe for her husband, captivated to tears as her daughter grows as a worship leader, or loudly cheering in one of the many basketball gyms across the East Coast watching her sons perfect their skills on the court. Some say this offers little time for herself, but Paris honestly would not want it any other way as her husband and children are her everything. However, when she does get a moment alone, it is usually spent in awe of God's work outdoors as she walks to find peace daily. Paris is a Lupus Advocate in support of her daughter and hopes to use her life's story of resilience to inspire others to transcend life's trials.

Contact Info.

Paris can be reached at: thewritevisionbyparis@gmail.com

Web: https://bit.ly/parisbrown

The Broken Widow God Restored

"God is married to the widows."

by Patricia Medley-Gibson

The Broken Widow God Restored

by Patricia Medley-Gibson

On August 10, 2007, my life changed. I did not think I would survive this storm, tragedy. I lost my best friend, my soul mate, the father of my child, my husband. The man I dated since I was 14 years old and the person, I have known most of my whole life, had passed away. I was lost and did not know which way to go.

I thank God for a praying, powerful woman named Marie Butler He placed in my life in 2000 she came up to the Hospital where me, my son and family were and prayed so hard for me as I was on the floor and out of it, feeling like everything was ripped from me. I did not want to be on earth anymore. I felt like I lost my everything. God said, "I am your everything. I am the Alpha and the Omega, the beginning and the end, the first and the last" (Revelation 22:13).

After God sent His angel to pray for me it felt like something had lifted me off the floor. I stood up and it was like God was telling me my son needed me. I realized I needed to get it together. There was still hope even in the midst of my brokenness, my hurt, my storm. After burying my first husband, I looked around at all the people that were there with me to help me get through before the funeral. After the funeral they were gone. I had to realize everybody had to go back to their normal lives. I felt like I was standing alone and all I could do was cry and God said, "I am right here my child, you are not alone. I will never leave nor forsake you." God is married to the widows. I tried going to counseling. I even took my son and it did not work. It seems like the pain and brokenness was getting worse. I ended up joining a church and began to get closer to God. I realize nobody could help me and my son but God. I prayed day and night. "The widow who is really in need and left alone puts her hope in God and continues night and day to pray and to ask God for help" (I Timothy 5:5 NIV). I went to every Bible study and would not miss one Bible study or church service on Sunday.

February 8th of 2008, I ended up in three different hospitals, having two different surgeries, an appendectomy, female problems, dealing with back pain, and sciatica nerve due to depression. I could not lay in bed or sit down or stand up due to being in so much pain. The pain was so unbearable. After one of my surgeries I was out of it and when I woke up, all my family was standing around me crying. I asked them what was wrong, I was good. They were worried because of the tragedy I had gone through losing my husband and going through grieving. I had battled with the back pain for 2 months which cost me to be out of work for 2-3 months. When God got me back on my feet this scripture was laid on my heart, "I can do all things through Christ who strengthens me" (Philippians 4:13 NKJV). "You intended to harm me, but God intended it for good to accomplish what is now being done..." (Genesis 50:20 NIV).

Being sick made me run after God even harder. And I realize faith in Christ is what I had to take to get that extra mile, to give me that strength to be carried just a bit further than I thought I was capable of. Through the years after all the grieving and suffering. God made me stronger and stronger. In 2010-2011 I fell off a little, started drinking, partying, and hanging out. But I would still get up on Sunday and go to church. I remember one night I went to a club and I knew I did not belong there. And have not looked back since. I repented and asked God to forgive me. I realized we may fall but we can get up. Getting up made me run after God even harder. I started working late hours at work so I could focus on the things that God wanted me to do and not what the world wanted me to do. I would get up every morning and read my Bible and pray. Lunch time, I would go to the lunchroom, read my Bible and pray, I would get off from work and go home at night, read my Bible and pray. I would do this almost every day.

A friend of mine came to my job and invited me to her church, I was currently attending another church in Prince Frederick. It was a 45-minute drive for me. She and I agreed if I go to her church she will come to my church. I ended up going to my friend's church first and my God, my God did the Holy Ghost show up and show out! Church was so powerful, and I heard God telling me this is your church. This is where you belong. We did not even make it back to the church I was attending.

I remember when people would ask me if I would ever get married again. I said, "No!" I always said that after my son graduated from high school and went off to college, I would travel with just God and me. But Lord behold, God had a different plan for me. God told me I would get married again. He said He would send me a God-fearing husband. God knows what is best for you more than you know yourself.

I would always sit in the back of the church with my mom and would hardly talk to anyone. I was quiet and stayed to myself. I was attending church one day when this man, Elder Gibson, came to me and asked if he could take me out for some tea (giggle). I was like *Tea*? I said, "Sure!" I was thinking he wanted to take me out to get me to talk and to connect with more people in the church. Lord behold he had another plan. He wanted to date me. I told him I was not ready to date at that time. I was focusing on God. I told him God will send him a wife as I stared him in his face. Underneath of my breath I was thinking it is not going to be me. (Laughing) He must have prayed hard because I tried to run, but it was like God kept pushing me back to him. He said he wanted to court me and that I was going to be his wife. I was like, I have to hear that from God myself. He said okay, but God already told me you are my wife, and He showed me in a dream. When he said this, I prayed and asked God to give me confirmation, and God would confirm that he is my husband. I kept saying, "nope" that is my not my husband.

One day during church service I fell in the Spirit and God said it again, "That is your husband and you need not to worry about what people think or say." As I was getting up from the floor, crying, and hearing God speaking to me. Two ladies were standing by me and as I was getting up from the floor (they couldn't hear what God spoke to me), one Lady said, "That is your husband." and the other lady said, "Don't worry about what people think or say." I started praising God again, and I was like, oh my God, God just spoke that in my spirit. That was confirmation! God told me, "I have work for you and your future husband to do." We ended up getting married 6 months later and have been married for 7 years.

"So, they are no longer two, but one flesh. Therefore, what God has joined together, let no one separate." We both love and praise the Lord together" (Matthew 19:6).

Pastor Margo's Heap of Hope

Lord, restore me! That has been the request of many believers who are seeking God's provision and repair. Unfortunately, many make this request not understanding that restoration is a process. Have you ever seen furniture being restored? Before it becomes that vintage, chic, desirable must-have, it is dirty, damaged, and frowned upon. Some of these classics are thrown to the curb outside and landfill bound. How do they become desirable? A tedious process of cleaning, sanding, scaping, and covering. Did you catch that? Before it can be lacquered it must be stripped of what it used to be. The residue of years of use, encounters with the atmosphere, and mishandling must be dealt with before it can be beautiful again. This process of restoration ensures that the nicks in the wood and the old coating do not prevent the new coating from shining brilliantly. It is only after going through this process that a beautiful coating is applied. It covers! It brings out the wood's age, beauty, and natural tones. This is the process God wants for you. He does not want a temporary coat of paint that hides blemishes. He wants to sand out those imperfections and create a glorious treasure who's worth has been increased by the process. Just as God restored the ruined cities for the children of Israel, God wants to restore you (Amos 9:14) Stay in the process, your transformation will be displayed soon enough. Let Him restore you (Psalm 51:12).

Patricia Medley-Gibson Bio

Patricia Medley-Gibson was born in Southern Maryland where she currently lives. Patricia worked in the medical field as a medical receptionist for 13 years. She attended University of Phoenix College in Greenbelt, Maryland for two years earning her Business Management Degree. Patricia stepped out on faith leaving the medical field behind and opened her own clothing boutique, Heavenly Fashion for All, LLC.

Patricia loves giving back to the community and being a blessing. She loves reading her Bible and spending time with her husband, Michael Gibson and her son, Delauntae Medley.

Contact Info.

Web: https://bit.ly/patriciamedleygibson

Captured Innocence

"His name was John."

by Laryssa Somerville

Captured Innocence

by Laryssa Somerville

He was extremely handsome. He stood about 6'4" tall, had a chocolate complexion, hazel brown eyes, and he reminded me of my favorite "Good Times" TV show character, James "Jay Jay" Evans, Jr., except he was more handsome. John could have played as Jay Jay's good-looking brother. I did not know how old he was exactly, probably in his early twenties. I knew he was too old to be messing with me, but he did not care and neither did I. I liked him and he liked me. I was so innocent until he captured my attention.

We were at my grandparent's house. I don't know where my uncle was, or why I was left alone with John, but he led me into my uncle's bedroom and laid me onto the bed. I remember laying there patiently waiting for him to remove my panties. He did not have to ask me; I automatically raised my hips so he could gently slide them down my legs. I was used to doing this because it was not my first time with him. I don't know how it started, but I do know that my innocent body felt different when John was around. It was a feeling I know as an adult meant I wanted him, but as a child, I could not explain it. I only knew I wanted to keep feeling this way. I know I could not keep my mind off him. I thought about him during class and I had thoughts about him touching me and me touching him. When we were together, he would whisper in my ear how beautiful and sexy I was to him. He would tell me how I tasted sweeter than any girl his age. Wow! No one had ever said such things to me. I thought about how much I liked sweets, and I giggled at the thought of being sweet to John. I was hooked early.

John was my uncle's best friend. He never asked me to keep our relationship a secret, but deep down inside I knew it was forbidden. I did not like seeing him around other girls. I would feel jealous when he joked around with my older, female cousins and would miss him on the days that he did not come around. He would never look at me when my uncles were near, but he would whisper, "I love you." or "I miss you." as soon as they turned their backs. John was my first love.

He took my panties and stuffed them into the front pocket of his shirt. He leaned over me and ever so gently kissed me in the center of my forehead and left the room. He left my dress up above my belly with my nakedness exposed. I fiddled with my dress. I pulled it down to cover myself, then raised it again, wanting to be pleasing to him. I would reposition my legs, first both parallel and straight, then one up with the knee bent. I really did not know what to do with myself when I had to wait for him. I wanted to be a big girl, but I could not grow up any faster.

He returned to the bedroom and I could tell by his smile that he was indeed pleased at the sight of me. He said I was beautiful and sexy. He loved my long red hair with natural highlights and my green eyes. He walked over to the bed and while standing, hovered his body over mine and kissed me again on the forehead. He brushed my hair from my eyes with the back of his hand and continued to tell me how beautiful I am and how he could not wait to take care of me. He told me I was ready. Maybe I was a big girl after all. He never laid beside me or on top of me. He kissed my belly, then explored my body as he spread my legs wide apart. I remember it felt so good, it would bring tears to my eyes. My heart would pound so hard, I could feel my pulse. My body would shake. This was like nothing I ever experienced. He would never disrobe, so I didn't know what his slim body looked like under his fitted t-shirt and jeans. Although he never penetrated me, my little body responded as if he had. He never did though because he said he wanted to keep me pure for when we got married.

This was our beautiful secret. Until one day, my uncle walked in on us. John was in his normal position, standing but hovering over me, with me laid on my back on the bed, eyes closed, and legs spread wide. I did not have a care in the world, and I didn't hear anything at first. As usual, all sounds were muffled to me while I was with John. Suddenly, I felt John stop as if he were being yanked away from me. I opened my eyes to see my uncle punching John in the face like a windmill. John appeared to be reaching for my uncle, who was visibly upset and yelling and punching, as they both lost their balance and fell to the floor from the blow after blow of punches my uncle was pounding him with. I sat up. I pulled my knees close and pulled my dress over my legs. I felt scared, mad, and confused. Why did my uncle come in here starting a fight with my lover anyway? My uncle's eyes were bloodshot red with rage. And why wouldn't John fight back? I wanted to stop my uncle from hurting my John, but I sat there frozen. Eventually I was able to hear clearly what my uncle was yelling. "What the **** are you doing man?!" John would not answer him at first.

I expected him to tell my uncle all the things he would say to me like, "I love her," and "she's beautiful" and reassure my uncle that he was going to marry me. But that did not happen. Instead John grabbed my uncle's arms and yelled back, "She asked me to do it. She wanted it." My uncle looked at me in disgust and with so much anger and hurt in his eyes. I could not say a word. I felt so embarrassed, neglected and more confused than ever. I still wanted John. My uncle stood over John, who was still lying on the floor protecting his face with his arms. He was breathing heavily with tears in his eyes and with a saliva filled mouth said, "What the **** do you mean? She's four-years-old." My uncle started kicking John. I wanted to protect him, but I could not move. I was frozen still. Soon, a couple of relatives rushed into the bedroom and pulled my uncle away from John. One of my aunts came in also and snatched me off the bed and carried me out of the room on her hip. No one ever asked me how I felt, and no one ever spoke of this again.

That would be the last time I would see John. He had captured my innocence, and now he was gone.

Stolen moments in a child's life often remain secrets wrapped in shame and left unnamed. Studies have shown that it is common for a child to experience their first memory as early as the age of three or four years old. Most children at this age enjoy singing, playing, and making up words. They may remember a school bus ride, an experience with a favorite teacher, a family meal, or a fun vacation. Sweet memories of innocent days can change the course of a life, but what happens when the memories have been tainted by a name? In my case, his name was, "John."

From this experience, I learned that memory suppression is real. For years I didn't understand certain triggers of emotions. Expressing myself through journaling was a great way to compartmentalize what I was feeling and put the puzzle pieces together to gauge what happened to me. God always sat me down, whispered to me to be still even when I didn't know the voice was from God. I know that throughout my life God always covered me. If you have a similar story, be encouraged. You are stronger than you realize

God revealed to me that I don't have to look like what I have been through. Make it your mission to fight with intention, every minute of the day to ensure that generational curses don't repeat themselves in your family. There is hope in leaning on His Word, and on His understanding. Wait on God and put your trust in Him.

Pastor Margo's Heap of Hope

There are many things in the kingdom that are considered taboo. Certain discussions are forbidden and "shushed" away as an annoyance. Such is the discussion of sexual abuse. Its evil hand is often hidden leaving its victims silenced and suffocating in their own tears. The Bible is not silent concerning the wickedness of these sins. Dinah the daughter of Jacob was raped by Shechem the son of a chief in the region (Genesis 34). This offended her brothers and fathers to the degree that it was punished with death. This is not noted to suggest that those who commit these crimes should be put to death (Romans 12:19), but to increase the awareness and demystify the horror of such acts.

As horrific as such acts are, you can live through it. You can be healed from it. You do not have to let it take up more of your life. You can give it to God. You can become a living testimony of God's healing power. Yes,

God can heal even that. He can heal the little girl and boy robbed of their innocence by someone who was supposed to love and care for them. He can heal the grown man or woman who has developed intimacy issues and fears it will happen again. He can remove the smell, the graphic memory, and the bitterness that creeps in when you feel robbed. As noted in Isaiah 43:2-3 when we go through the deep waters, God will be there. When we go through rivers of difficulty, we will not drown. Even when we walk through the fire of oppression, we will not be burned up and the flames will not consume you. Run into God's arms. You can find rest (Matthew 11:28). He will not let this consume you and will not let you down in it. Run in!

Laryssa Somerville Bio

Laryssa Somerville is a devoted wife, mother, and grandmother, and the sole proprietor of several businesses; Essence Beauty and Barber Salon in both Lexington Park and Waldorf MD; Executive Salon Suites and The Pink Zebra Kids Spa in Lexington Park, as well as Hairstuff.com. She adds to her repertoire serving on the Praise and Worship team at The Remnant of Hope International Church where Pastor Margo Gross is her spiritual covering, and often ministers through song at funerals and weddings locally. In her spare time, Laryssa can be found sewing, crocheting, swimming, bike riding, and motorcycling as she seeks to live healthy.

Web: https://bit.ly/laryssasomerville

My Story, My Mess, God's Masterpiece

"*God let me know that He loved me.*"

by Patrice Brooks

My Story, My Mess, God's Masterpiece

by Patrice Brooks

"Oh my gosh, I'm late," I said to myself in the mirror. I was scared. What was wrong with me? I knew I had "female issues," but was that the reason my period was late?! I also knew that I was very sexually active with my boyfriend of almost two years. But I did not think it was that and when I told him, he had this wide-eyed expression. He asked me if I thought I was, and I told him I did not know. In early June of 2005 after midnight, we went to the only grocery store that was open outside of the neighborhoods we both grew up in. We picked out three pregnancy tests and went back to his aunt's house and took them. They all came back negative. "Whew," he said as he kissed me on my cheek. However, I did not feel any relief. I was panicking inside because I knew there was a chance, I could still be pregnant.

As a young woman who had grown up in church since a baby, I knew fornicating was wrong. Even after my first time, I cried and repented to God. But somewhere along the way, the conviction was not as strong, and I kept making excuses for my behavior. Within two weeks, it was confirmed. I was pregnant. There was a plethora of emotions that I experienced. And six months and two days after my 20th birthday, I became a mother to a handsome son. About a year and a half later, I graduated from college with honors and it was time to face the real world. A year after that, my son's father and I decided that we would co-parent for the sake of our son.

For a couple of years, I lived hard for God. I wanted companionship, but I was not willing to risk my relationship with God. But then came an old flame. An old flame, who was in church and was just getting out of a relationship himself. We connected on a friendship level and then things turned quickly. Just as quickly as they had heated up, they fizzled out. I never had a true commitment from him. I so wanted this situation to work, but realistically it was going nowhere fast. Not long after the entanglement ended, he got married. It was a chin check, a gut punch, a proverbial slap in the face. I tried to pick up the pieces and really go hard for God. However, a few years later, I found myself in two more "situationships," as I like to call them. They were different people at different times, but it was a familiar scenario. They were familiar to me, people I had grown up with, gone to school and/or church with, people who I felt I could trust. In each situationship, it seemed as though I had connected with each of them on a "spiritual" level, trying to prove that I was not as carnal minded as I had been the time before. But truth be told, I was more carnal each time because I was trying to fill a void.

I tried to fill a void with companionship and even idolizing marriage at one point because I felt as though I was missing out. I felt like I needed to give something up to get something in return. And I was. I was giving a piece of myself, of my soul, to each partner. I was dying a slow spiritual death because I felt inadequate. I felt I needed validation. I just did not want to be alone. I wanted to feel I belonged to someone.

After the last situationship ended, I was the most devastated I had ever been. I really thought I connected with this guy. We had so many things in common. We visited each other's churches, we did devotionals together each week, I supported him in his endeavors and I just knew this was starting to be something. But as quickly as we had connected spiritually, we had connected physically, and we both felt so bad. I just knew he was the one, y'all hear me? As soon as I started feeling a way, the rug was pulled out from under me. He started to pull away and I started to feel like, "What have I done? Was there something I could do better? Do I talk too much? Did I give too much attitude about something and turn him off? How can I be better?" (These questions are not wrong to ask, but should I have been asking myself the questions in relation to a man? The answer is no. We should always want to be better and see how we can handle things differently, but not because we are trying to impress someone other than God.) As time went on, he and I drifted further apart, but not without those confusing text messages and phone calls. Those times included me listening to his woes and offering encouragement because after all that is just who I am, I would tell myself. I was too available and accessible. The last conversation I had with him I was listening to him tell me while he was in a drunken state that he appreciated me, and he needed me. I felt like maybe he was coming back around. But not long after that conversation, I heard he was engaged. Our mutual friends were too afraid to tell me and I lashed out at them. I wanted to blame them for how dumb I felt. A few months after, on my way to my best friend's house, as I drove past the courthouse courtyard, I saw a wedding and I knew it was them. It was the day after my birthday and my heart shattered into pieces. It was after this ordeal that I really had to sit down and deal with me.

That earth-shattering event sent me into a spiral of depression. I kept asking myself why this was happening to me? Why was it happening again? Was there something wrong with me? I even asked my close friends if I had imagined him liking me as much as I thought. I just felt so abandoned. I felt unloved, undesired, unwanted. I began to gain weight again. I began to struggle at work, at church, as a mother. It affected every area of my life, but I tried to put on a happy face. I tried to live behind the façade that everything was okay because I am a Christian. I'm supposed to have it all together, right? I silently condemned myself. I felt misused and mishandled. I felt like I had discounted myself and that I deserved what I received because I was so stupid. But thank God for His grace.

I don't really know when it changed for me. It was not a date on the calendar I could mark to say that that was the day I needed to allow God in to show me, me. It was gradual or should I say it has been gradual. It has been several years since the incident and this is what I have learned. I learned that I had to be real with myself and I had to be honest with God because He knows how I feel anyway. I began to ask myself how I had ended up in similar situations with different people. I mean the common denominator was me. I did not want to be the victim anymore. I did not need to go and ask other people or seek their validation anymore. I needed my Daddy. I needed my Heavenly Father, Jesus. I began to talk with Him.

It was during those times that I realized I had Daddy issues. I had Mommy issues. I felt abandoned by the two people, who I needed the most. I realized that because of these situations and the circumstances of life, I felt I needed to be needed by people. My feelings of inadequacy did not just start because of a failed relationship or four. It started because I blamed myself for my parent's divorce. I was an honor student, but I felt I should do better in school. I felt that it was my responsibility. I know it seems silly for a child to have those feelings, but I did. It was a situation I could not control. So, I went on to have these relationships with various men searching for validation, searching for love, searching for the things I did not feel like I received because of the divorce. Looking back at those relationships, I realized I was broken. I realized that I had carried that brokenness of my adolescent self into every relationship I had. And from each relationship, I gave my peace away and gained more brokenness. The truth was that I also idolized marriage and maybe that was because my parents' marriage didn't work. Looking back, I know I felt a way about not being able to control what happened with my parents. I felt that I would be able to control my own timetable and destiny when it came to marriage. I wanted to feel loved so badly that I was willing to settle in those earlier situations. Somewhere along the way, I did not feel good enough about who God said I was. But it was imperative to my life, to my son's life for me to be free and for God to take this mess and make it into a masterpiece.

From an early age, there were various people who said things like I was a leader and that I would do great things for God. I remember at the age of 11, I ministered for the first time at a Youth Sunday service. I have always felt comfortable behind the microphone speaking. I always wondered why that was. I wondered why I did not really possess the same shyness others had when speaking to a room of people. My mother made sure I was well spoken and used proper grammar. As the years went on, I even realized I had a knack for listening to people and being an encourager. But with having experienced those moments, I still did not feel I was good enough for God.

I felt that I had failed Him because of what I had done and what I had allowed myself to be subjected to. But God through His infinite wisdom began having me read His Word, listen to His preached Word, and grow closer to Him in worship. He even transitioned me out of what I had known for years into a place of refuge and of hope. God dealt with me in a very real way. I had to stop pointing the fingers at everything and everyone else and look at three fingers pointing back at me. I could no longer use these situations as a crutch to continue to play the victim. I had to fight. I had to fight my way back to the peace God had given me. I had to fight my way back to who God said I was separate and apart from a relationship. I had to truly commune with God and stop putting on a façade because He knows who I am and what I have done anyway. I really wanted to be healed, delivered, and set free. But I needed to stop running from the truth.

I needed to allow God to speak His truth to me. I needed God to let me know I was valuable to Him and that no one else needed to validate me. God let me know that He loved me. He let me know that He cared. God began to heal my heart. He began to change my mindset about myself. He continues to guide me in those things because I matter to Him. One of my favorite scriptures is Jeremiah 29:11, which states, "For I know the plans I have for you," declares the LORD, "plans to prosper you and not to harm you, plans to give you hope and a future" (NIV). I held on and still hold onto that scripture along with several others like:

"Before I formed you in the womb, I knew you, before you were born, I set you apart" (Jeremiah 1:5a, NIV).

"And we know that all things work together for good to them that love God, to them who are the called according to his purpose" (Romans 8:28, KJV).

"Rejoice in the Lord always: and again, I say, rejoice.5 Let your moderation be known unto all men. The Lord is at hand.6 Be careful for nothing; but in every thing by prayer and supplication with thanksgiving let your requests be made known unto God.7 And the peace of God, which passeth all understanding, shall keep your hearts and minds through Christ Jesus.8 Finally, brethren, whatsoever things are true, whatsoever things are honest, whatsoever things are just, whatsoever things are pure, whatsoever things are lovely, whatsoever things are of good report; if there be any virtue, and if there be any praise, think on these things.9 Those things, which ye have both learned, and received, and heard, and seen in me, do: and the God of peace shall be with you.10 But I rejoiced in the Lord greatly, that now at the last your care of me hath flourished again; wherein ye were also careful, but ye lacked opportunity.11 Not that I speak in respect of want: for I have learned, in whatsoever state I am, therewith to be content.12 I know both how to be abased, and I know how to abound: everywhere and in all things I am instructed both to be full and to be hungry, both to abound and to suffer need.13 I can do all things through Christ which strengtheneth me" (Philippians 4:4-13, KJV).

2 My brethren, count it all joy when ye fall into divers temptations;3 Knowing this, that the trying of your faith worketh patience.4 But let

patience have her perfect work, that ye may be perfect and entire, wanting nothing (James 1:2-4, KJV).

I knew with these scriptures and so many more that I could make it through these trials. I knew that even when the going got tough, I had God and He was truly all I needed. I had to go through those situations because I needed to fully rely on God. He needed me to draw closer to Him. I was in a backslidden state, not just with my body, but in my heart. When I jumped out there in these relationships, I let God know that I did not trust Him. I did not check with Him to make sure I was supposed to engage with those men at all. I did my own thing. I created my own mess. But God never condemned me. He wanted me to see that He is in control and always has my best interests at heart.

Going through these situations taught me and is still teaching me a lot about myself. It taught me that I did not have to put myself on the clearance rack. It taught me the value of who Patrice is. It also taught me that I want to teach my son the right way to treat women and to always be honest even if it hurts. It taught me that God is sovereign, and He reigns. He is the God who sees me. He is the God who knew I would make mistakes, knew I would not fully trust Him, knew I feared being alone and abandoned and He still chose me. God knew all I would go through as a child and throughout adulthood. He knew that His daughter would falter, but He was right there to pick me up.

By the time this book is released, it will have been a little over a year since I have been behind the microphone saying what God would have me to say. It amazes me that He chose me. I think back to those words spoken over me as a child and beyond and it encourages me that God will do just what He said He would do. When I think about my story, I am humbled. I see God's hand in every way. He has and is healing me from the inside out. My confidence in Him is steadily building. The beautiful thing is that God did not let me become jaded about love and marriage. I still desire marriage, but it does not consume me or lead my decisions. I still love, love. I still see the beauty in love and marriage. I can appreciate the sanctity of marriage more and appreciate why God instituted it in the first place. It is a holy union, a purposeful union that must (or at least should) take place at the right time. I am confident that God knows my desires and I trust His timing is perfect. I have grown to understand that He knows all and sees all. So, the rejection I once felt was His protection. I am so thankful that He protected my heart even when I did not want Him to, even when I did not understand.

I have been single for eight years. Eight years not in a situationship. Eight years not selling myself short. Eight years of healing and communing with my Heavenly Father. I have a better relationship with both of my parents as a result. I thank Him for seeing me. I thank God for taking this mess, my mess, and making it into a masterpiece. The coolest thing is, He is not even finished yet! I am excited to see all He will do not just in my life, but in your lives too! Remember that God sees you and He cares. No matter what has happened in your past, God can give you "beauty for ashes." Allow Him to heal you, guide you and make you whole. Singlehood is a blessing. Do not let your own timetable or even the timetable of others make you forget that everything is made perfect in God's timing. Let the Master take the pieces of your life and make them into a masterpiece exuding the Master's peace!

Pastor Margo's Heap of Hope

The enemy does not want us to know who we are. If we ever really discover exactly who we are in God we would value not just ourselves, but our time. We would change how we live. We would not accept anything. We would protect our spirit. Many of our poor decisions, impulses, and just flat out regrets are felt in connection with our identities. Not what people call us, but what we believe about ourselves. David is an example of someone who knew who he was. After making a kind gesture of taking care of Nabal's sheep, David requested provisions (bread and water) in return. He sent his servants in peace. However, Nabal's response was, "Who is David and who is the son of Jesse?" (I Samuel 15:10). Nabal did not value David, know who he was, or honor David's request. David did not argue, he merely showed him exactly who he was, a fierce warrior. Our job is not to argue with the enemy nor spend time sulking over someone else's estimate of our worth. We are to simply act like who we are, whose we are, and move in the power of our identity. The bible calls us a chosen generation, a royal priesthood, a holy nation, and peculiar people (I Peter 2:9). Take a quick evaluation of your circle, circumstances, and decisions. Were they the decisions of royalty? Do your decisions reflect those of someone chosen by God? If not, it's time do what the prodigal son did and "come to yourself" (Luke 15: 17). The prodigal son realized who his father was and what he was giving away. He turned back to his father. Do it today! Walk in your royalty. Take your rightful seat as a child of the most high God.

Patrice Brooks Bio

Patrice Brooks is a first-time author and has always been an avid reader. She is a graduate of the University of Maryland Eastern Shore with a Bachelor's in Rehabilitation Services. She is the mother of one son, who is the light of her life and who keeps her busy. When Patrice is not reading or keeping up with her son's many activities, she is planning events through her own event planning business, Patrice & Co. She loves God and her family. Patrice desires to tell the world about Jesus and share her story to help others. Patrice currently lives in Maryland.

Contact Info.

Web: https://bit.ly/patricebrooks

I'm Still Here by the Grace of God

"The stories I could tell you . . ."

by Katrina Thomas

I'm Still Here by the Grace of God

by Katrina Thomas

I was raised in a strict Baptist home. I was in church all the time and was sheltered and not allowed to do things that most teenagers did.

I met a young man in my Senior year of High School who was the opposite of me. I think that is what attracted me to him, and why at the age of eighteen years old we got married. I was a virgin when we got married and knew absolutely nothing about sex but, was in love.

In the early years of our marriage I was treated like a queen, but that turned into him being very controlling and possessive. That is when the abuse started. I walked around on eggshells all the time trying to make sure things were perfect when he came home. He started drinking very heavily after losing his job that he loved, and I never knew how he would come home. I was physically and mentally abused all the time and even left him, but I always went back. By this time, I had three children and felt helpless without him. After leaving the third time and sleeping at friends I left for good.

What I neglected to say was along the way he introduced me to weed. From weed to cocaine and we partied that way a lot. I found that to cope with the abuse being high helped me to cope. Once I left him though I realized I enjoyed that lifestyle. It was glamorizing because I partied with middle class drug users. Such as Doctors, lawyers, hairdressers, and it felt like it was okay. I would leave home sometimes to a place and what was supposed to be one night turned into three. My children were often left to care for themselves. At times they would call their grandparents to pick them up.

The stories I could tell you about that lifestyle is crazy to even think about today. I struggled with working and how to stop using. I knew it was something I had to get a grip on. I tried to commit suicide three times because of feeling so hopeless. I enjoyed getting high but knew it was killing me. Crazy right! My family was trying to help me, but the struggle was so real, and I thought I could stop anytime.

There was one night I went to get drugs from this guy and later after I left, someone called me to say people came in to rob him. They tied him, his wife and child up and put guns to their heads. You would think this would make me want to stop. The lifestyle of a drug user can be life threatening, and I never thought I had hit what people say was my bottom. I was not homeless and still managed to work. Waking up in places not remembering how I got there really scared me though. I could not make it to work even though it was nothing bad like being robbed, or physically hurt.

Using drugs, I found, causes one to be very selfish. I only thought of myself. One day I had a serious conversation with my dad who also was a recovering alcoholic, who told me I needed to want better for myself and not do what he did. He convinced me to go into rehab. Wondering how in the world I was going to make it without drugs and alcohol which was my go-to everyday. I struggled to go to the hospital, but I did. I had to sign papers to give guardianship to my sister to care for my youngest daughter. It broke my heart to do it, but I had to be better for me to be better for my children. I was in rehab for six months and moved with my parents. God knows I did not want to do that either, but I had to separate myself from those people, places, and things that could pull me back in. Some people do not have that option and when they get out of rehab they have to go back to an environment where drugs and drinking is still being done.

Well, I started going back to church with a family member. I had tried before but always returned to drinking and often went to church smelling of alcohol. Trying to hide it with perfume, sprays, and mouthwash.

I was not using drugs but would still drink here and there. One night at a prayer service I stood up to give my testimony. I cannot believe I did that, but I cried out to God to help me. I had never done that before. I knew there was a God but, never taught relationship in my old church. So when I broke down and cried out to God I had no idea what was going to happen but I knew I was sick and tired of being sick and tired and wanted to stop using just as much as I wanted to use. I opened myself up to God. To this day I cannot explain it but, God delivered me at that moment.

I stayed with my parents, got a job, and went back to church and learned more about who God is and how he alone helped me through the process of deliverance. I even started a support group. It was rough but I developed a personal relationship with God. I stood on one scripture (Ps.37) through my process of staying connected to God (His Word).

I am here to tell someone some of my many stories and that I know the struggle is real, but God is able to do exceedingly and above all that we could imagine.

I thought I would die in my addiction but, with God, supportive family, and friends I found my way back.

The struggle is real and different for everyone, but God saved my life. I did not abort the process and I'm so glad to be here today to share my testimony of overcoming a physically abusive relationship and drugs.

To God be all the Glory for the things that He has done.

In Memory of Marchelle

Pastor Margo's Heap of Hope

To conquer means to subdue until resistance is no longer made, to overcome, win, and to gain by force. The Bible tells us in Romans 8:37 that we are more than conquerors through Him who loved us. We were born again to overcome and win. We were not created to live in defeat. In fact, the bible also tells us God always causes us to triumph in Christ. The victory has already been won. We only need to run by faith to the finish line to claim the prize God already has for us. Life attempts to distract us with a view of defeat, whisper losing confirmations, and show us who appears to be out-running us, but things are not always what they seem. God is always at work. We only need to continue the race to see victory.

Conquerors understand that the presence of resistance or deterrents are not causes to retreat or turn back. When faced with resistance, conquerors pursue and apply pressure until resistance can no longer be made. They gain victory often by force. For it to be a victory it must be achieved with resistance. If you are feeling resistance, maintain your stride. Keep your pace! Do not look to your left or right. Look to the hills and cross that finish line. The Lord is with you and your victory is inevitable.

Katrina Thomas Bio

Katrina Thomas is a native of Washington, DC, and an Anacostia High School graduate. She is a licensed cosmetologist having done hair for 35 years. Katrina also received an associate degree in Christian Education. She is currently an Elder at Remnant of Hope International Church under the leadership of her daughter, Pastor Margo Gross. In earlier churches, Katrina was the minister of the Singles Ministry and led the New Members' Classes. Now, at Remnant, she oversees the Armor Bearers, the Finance, and New Members ministries.

Katrina is the mother of three beautiful girls, Marsha, Marchelle, and Margo; grandma to three: Robert, Ariyanna, and Samiah; and great grandma to Connor and one more due soon.

Katrina loves to mentor women, especially those who struggle with things she has overcome. She gives all the glory to God for saving her life.

Contact Info.

Web: https://bit.ly/katrinathomas

Virgins and Unicorns

"Apparently, virgins nowadays are like unicorns."

by LaKesha L. Williams

Virgins and Unicorns

by LaKesha L. Williams

"Hello, my name is LaKesha and I am a virgin."

There was a time in my life when I would not have told people I was a virgin. There was even a time that I lied about being a virgin just to fit in and not feel awkward or appear inexperienced. Here is the thing though; being a virgin is not something that I should have been ashamed of for any reason. Let me pause and be clear, I am not condemning anyone who is not currently a virgin. This is my walk and I am simply sharing my story.

You know how sometimes new books that are purchased from a bookstore often come in shrink-wrapped packaging, and the stipulation is that once you open the package you cannot return the book. Well, this is how virginity is—particularly my virginity. Admittedly, I have some fingerprints on my packaging, however no one has opened the packaging yet. The only person who can open the package at this point is the one who has paid the price for it. That price is called marriage!

In 1 Corinthians 6:18-20 (NLT) the Bible says, "Flee from sexual immorality. Every other sin a person commits is outside the body, but the sexually immoral person sins against his own body. Or do you not know that your body is a temple of the Holy Spirit within you, whom you have from God? You are not your own, for you were bought with a price. So, glorify God in your body."

I am 37 years old and still a virgin. I am not ashamed, or what I really should say is, I am no longer ashamed. I am grateful for all that I have been protected from by still being a virgin. I am grateful for the ways of escape God has provided for me when I have placed myself in "hot & heavy" situations where the course of my life could have changed, and I would not be able to write this today. I just want to encourage you today that your life is not about you. I have discovered that everything that has ever happened in my life only enhanced my testimony that I have been tasked to share to encourage others to overcome and win souls for Christ. You will experience so much freedom once you realize this. Being a virgin, is nothing to hide. I will scream it from the mountain tops only to give God the glory. As unashamed as you are about sharing other things (on Social Media sites, or in conversation with friends and family), be that unashamed about sharing your faith and your testimony to help others overcome and ignite hope! Being a virgin is something that is sacred and special. I often compare being a virgin to seeing a unicorn.

A unicorn is believed to be this mythical creature that resembles a white horse with a horn on its head. In allegories, they are believed to be a real but very rare and magical creature. Unicorns supposedly represent harmony and purity and all things good. Apparently, virgins nowadays are like unicorns. Again, I am 37 years old and I am a virgin. I am not ashamed. I no longer feel like I am missing out on anything, and I am grateful that God has sustained and continues to sustain me to wait until marriage.

However, when I am talking to people and sharing my story with them, I sometimes leave the conversation feeling like a unicorn. Some of the responses I get are hilarious and some are heartbreaking:

"Girl, I don't know how you do it!"

"Seriously?!"

"So, are you saying you never ever had sex?"

"You should try it. You might like it…"

"What are you waiting for?"

The list could go on and on, I believe at this point in my life I probably have heard every response there is both encouraging to downright rude. Ultimately with believers and non-believers it is heartbreaking to see that something that should be regarded as sacred really is not anymore. Again, one of the responses I have heard is, "What you are waiting for?" This is probably the top one, so here are my top three answers to this infamous question:

My number one reason for waiting until marriage to have sex is: I want to honor God with my body. In 1 Corinthians 6:19-20 we are told that our bodies are not our own so we cannot give away what doesn't belong to us. What did Paul mean when he said that our bodies belong to God? Many people say they have the right to do whatever they want with their own bodies. Although they think that this is freedom, they are really enslaved to their own desires. When we become Christians, the Holy Spirit fills, and lives in us. Therefore, we no longer own our bodies. "Bought with a price" refers to slaves purchased at auction. Christ's death freed us from sin, but also binds us to His service. If you are living in a building owned by someone else, you try not to violate the building's rules. Because your body belongs to God, you must not violate His standards for living.

Having sex before marriage is stealing, and you are taking something that does not belong to you; and you have not paid the price for. Our lives are not our own, so again I call attention to another part in 1 Corinthians 6:19-20 where it says, "You are not your own." The scripture says, "you were bought with a price." When you go into a store and you see something you want, do you just take it? No, you do not, because taking something that you have not paid for is called stealing! Instead, you either do one of two things—You pay for it or you work hard and save your money to pay for it later. We were created to worship God, to be loved by God; and having sex before marriage is worshipping ourselves, gratifying our fleshly desires and exalting our flesh and the things of this world above a loving, merciful and sovereign God. Someone may be reading this thinking, "Wow, she is really going in!" Well, yes, I am because the Word of God is real and it is true and it is the only thing I have to rely on, so why wouldn't I live by and apply all that God has commanded me in His Word? So, to enhance my first reason I want to honor God with my body and keep His commands.

My second reason for waiting until marriage to have sex is: I do not want to suffer the mental and emotional heartache, headache and drama that comes with having premarital sex. Sex is a beautiful thing, sex is great, and sex is wonderful, how do I know? I know because the Bible tells me so! However outside of marriage sex can be complicated. The act of having sex is not just physical; the act of sexual intercourse is physical, mental, emotional, and spiritual, it is all-encompassing.

Genesis 2:24 (NLT) says, "For this reason a man shall leave his father and his mother and be joined to his wife; and they shall become one flesh."

God gave marriage as a gift to Adam and Eve. They were created perfect for each other. Marriage was not just for convenience, nor was it brought about by any culture. It was instituted by God and has three basic aspects: (1) The man leaves his parents and, in a public act, promises himself to his wife; (2) the man and woman are joined together by taking responsibility for each other's welfare and by loving the mate above all others; (3) the two become one flesh in the intimacy and commitment of sexual union that is reserved for marriage. Strong marriages include all three of these aspects.

In an article I read about marriage, it broke this verse down like this: "When the Bible says that two shall become one flesh, more is meant than what we would mean by the phrase, physical union. Man, as flesh includes his spirit and soul because he is living flesh due to having a spirit and in being a living soul. The word flesh refers to his entire nature. The biblical understanding of man as flesh shows that the sexual union is not simply a union of two bodies as if the bodies were separate from the souls of the two persons." I am about my Father's Business and to be Kingdom minded I do not have time to be caught up in my feelings about a man that I have slept with who is not my husband. Which brings me to another point:

Premarital sex is a distraction and pulls us away from the will of God for our lives, it pulls us away from our purpose because we are too busy thinking about who we are sleeping with and what they are doing to be focused on the things of God and advancing the Kingdom of God.

My third reason for waiting until marriage to have sex is: I do not want to have a child out of wedlock, and I do not want to contract any diseases or infections. I really do not think I need to elaborate much on this reason because it is self-explanatory. If you have not had sex yet, don't. Eliminate and flee from temptation. Ask God to sustain you and wait until marriage. If you have had sex or engaged in sexual activity with yourself or someone else, cry out to God with a repentant heart, confess, repent and rededicate your body to God, eliminate and flee from temptation and ask Him to sustain you until marriage. We serve a loving, merciful and forgiving God who sent his Son Jesus to die on the cross for all of us, and it is never too late for anyone to come back home to the arms of Jesus!

The unicorn analogy was a lighthearted approach to a serious issue. Virgins do exist, I know a few and we believe in honoring God with our bodies. No, we are not perfect, and yes, we sometimes fall short, but God's grace and mercy are both sufficient for us! Being a virgin is not easy, but I know it will certainly be worth it!

Below you will find two prayers from Ransomed Heart Ministries. One is a Prayer for Sexual Healing; the second is a Prayer to Break Soul Ties.

A Prayer for Sexual Healing

Healing for your sexuality is available; this is a very hopeful truth! But you must realize that your sexuality is deep and core to your nature as a human being. Therefore, sexual brokenness can be one of the deepest types of brokenness a person might experience. You must take your healing and restoration seriously. This guided prayer will help immensely.

You may find you need to pray through it a few times to experience a lasting freedom.

A bit of explanation on the reasons for the prayer: first, when we misuse our sexuality through sin, we give Satan an open door to oppress us in our sexuality. A man who uses pornography will find himself in a very deep struggle with lust; a woman who was sexually promiscuous before marriage may find herself wrestling with sexual temptation years afterward. So, it is important to bring our sexuality under the lordship (and therefore protection) of the Lord Jesus Christ and seek his cleansing of our sexual sins.

Second, sexual brokenness—whether through abuse of our sexuality by our own actions or by the actions of others—can create sexual difficulties and opens the door for the enemy to oppress us. Quite often forgiveness is needed—both the confidence that we are forgiven by the Lord and the choice we make to forgive others. This will prove immensely freeing.

Let us begin by bringing our lives and sexuality under the lordship of Jesus Christ:

> *Lord Jesus Christ, I confess here and now that you are my Creator (John 1:3) and therefore the creator of my sexuality. I confess that you are also my Savior, that you have ransomed me with your blood (1 Corinthians 15:3, Matthew 20:28). I have been bought with the blood of Jesus Christ; my life and my body belong to God (1 Corinthians 6:19–20). Jesus, I present myself to you now to be made*

whole and holy in every way, including in my sexuality. You ask us to present our bodies to you as living sacrifices (Romans 12:1) and the parts of our bodies as instruments of righteousness (Romans 6:13). I do this now. I present my body, my sexuality ["as a man" or "as a woman"] and I present my sexual nature to you. I consecrate my sexuality to Jesus Christ.

Next, you need to renounce the ways you have misused your sexuality. The more specific you can be, the more helpful this will be. God created your sexuality for pleasure and joy within the context of the marriage covenant. Sexual activity outside of marriage can be very damaging to a person and to their relationships (1 Corinthians 6:18–20). What you want to do in this part of the prayer is confess and renounce all sexual sin—for example, sexual intimacy outside of marriage, not only intercourse, but other forms of sexual intimacy such as mutual masturbation or oral sex. Many people assume these "don't really count as sin" because they did not result in actual intercourse; however, there was sexual stimulation and intimacy outside marriage. Keep in mind there is the "spirit of the law" and the "letter of the law." What matters are issues of heart and mind as well as body. Other examples of sins to renounce would be extramarital affairs, the use of pornography, and sexual fantasies. You may know exactly what you need to confess and renounce; you may need to ask God's help to remember. Take your time here. As memories and events come to mind, confess, and renounce them. For example: "Lord Jesus, I ask your forgiveness for my sins of masturbation and using pornography. I renounce those sins in your name." After you have confessed your sins, go on with the rest of the prayer.

Jesus, I ask your Holy Spirit to help me now remember, confess, and renounce my sexual sins. [Pause. Listen. Remember. Confess and renounce.] Lord Jesus, I ask your forgiveness for every act of sexual sin. You promised that if we confess our sins, you are faithful and just to forgive us our sins and cleanse us from all unrighteousness (1 John 1:9). I ask you to cleanse me of my sexual sins now; cleanse my body, soul, and spirit, cleanse my heart and mind and will, cleanse my sexuality. Thank you for forgiving me and cleansing me. I receive your forgiveness and cleansing. I renounce every claim I have given Satan to my life or sexuality through my sexual sins. Those claims are now broken by the cross and blood of Jesus Christ (Colossians 2:13–15).

Next comes forgiveness. It is vital that you forgive both yourself and those who have harmed you sexually. LISTEN CAREFULLY. Forgiveness is a choice. We often have to make the decision to forgive long before we feel forgiving. We realize this can be difficult, but the freedom you will find will be worth it! Forgiveness is not saying, "It didn't hurt me." Nor is forgiveness saying, "It didn't matter." Forgiveness is the act whereby we pardon the person; we release them from all bitterness and judgment. We give them to God to deal with.

Lord Jesus, I thank you for offering me total and complete forgiveness. I receive that forgiveness now. I choose to forgive myself for all my sexual wrongdoing. I also choose to forgive those who have harmed me sexually. [Be specific here; name those people and forgive them.] I release them to you. I release all my anger and judgment toward them. Come, Lord Jesus, into the pain they caused me, and heal me with your love.

This next step involves breaking the unhealthy emotional and spiritual bonds formed with other people through sexual sin. One of the reasons the Bible takes sexual sin so seriously is because of the damage it does. Another reason is because of the bonds it forms with people—bonds meant to be formed only between husband and wife (see 1 Corinthians 6:15–20). One of the marvelous effects of the cross of our Lord Jesus Christ is that it breaks these unhealthy bonds. "May I never boast except in the cross of our Lord Jesus Christ, through which the world has been crucified to me and I to the world" (Galatians 6:14).

I now bring the cross of my Lord Jesus Christ between me and every person with whom I have been sexually intimate. [Name them specifically whenever possible. Also name those who have abused you sexually.] I break all sexual, emotional, and spiritual bonds with [name if possible, or just "that girl in high school" if you cannot remember her name]. I keep the cross of Christ between us.

Many people experience negative consequences through the misuse of their sexuality. Those consequences might be lingering guilt (even after confession) or repeated sexual temptation. Consequences might also be the inability to enjoy sex with their spouse. It will help to bring the work of Christ here as well. Many people end up making unhealthy "agreements" about sex or themselves, about men or women or intimacy, because of the damage they have experienced through sexual sin (their sin, or the sin of someone against them). You will want to ask Christ what those agreements are and break them!

Lord Jesus, I ask you to reveal to me every "agreement" I have made about my sexuality or this specific struggle. [An example would be "I will always struggle with this" or "I can never get free" or "I don't deserve to enjoy sex now" or "My sexuality is dirty." Pause and let Jesus reveal those agreements to you. Then break them.] I break this agreement [name it] in the name of my Lord Jesus Christ, and I renounce every claim I have given it in my life. I renounce [name what the struggle is— "the inability to have an orgasm" or "this lingering shame" or "the hatred of my body"]. I bring the cross and blood of Jesus Christ against this [guilt or shame, every negative consequence]. I banish my enemy from my sexuality in the mighty name of the Lord Jesus Christ. I invite the healing presence of Jesus Christ to cleanse me and restore me as a sexual being in fullness of joy and wholeness. I ask you, Jesus, to fill my sexuality with your holiness, to strengthen me and restore me in your name.

Finally, it will prove helpful to consecrate your sexuality to Jesus Christ once more.

Lord Jesus, I now consecrate my sexuality to you in every way. I consecrate my sexual intimacy with my spouse to you. I ask you to cleanse and heal my sexuality and our sexual intimacy in every way. I ask your healing grace to come and free me from all consequences of sexual sin. I ask you to fill my sexuality with your healing love and goodness. Restore my sexuality in wholeness. Let my spouse and me experience all the intimacy and pleasure you intended a man and woman to enjoy in marriage. I invite the Spirit of God to fill our marriage bed. I pray all of this in the name of Jesus Christ, my Lord. Amen!!

We could report many, many stories of stunning redemption that have come because of individuals and couples praying through this type of prayer. Now remember—sometimes the wounds and consequences take time to heal. You might want to revisit this prayer several times over if lasting healing has not yet taken place. You may recall actions that need confession later; return to this prayer and confess those as well. Some of you will also receive help from seeing a good Christian counselor. Hold fast to these truths:

You, your body, and your sexuality belong to Jesus Christ. He has completely forgiven you. He created your sexuality to be whole and holy. He created your sexuality to be a source of intimacy and joy. Jesus Christ came to seek and save "what was lost" (Luke 19:10), including all that was lost in the blessings he intended through our sexuality!

A Prayer for Breaking Soul Ties

I bring the cross of my Lord Jesus Christ between me and [name this person]. As Galatians 6:14 says, I have been crucified to [name them], and they have been crucified to me. So, by the cross of Jesus Christ, I break every soul tie and every unholy bond with [name them]. I command their human spirit bound back to their body, and I send all their sin and warfare and corruption bound back to the throne of Christ in their life. I forbid them or their warfare or their sin to transfer to me. And I allow only the love of God, only the bond of the Holy Spirit, between us. In the name of my Lord Jesus Christ. Amen.

Pastor Margo's Heap of Hope

Standing takes effort, balance, and the support of a sure foundation. Sitting is easy it is one of the first positions babies learn how to position themselves in. Over time babies begin to use them to pull themselves up and then hold on for support. The same is true for our walk with God. We must stand, even when the world we live in believes our principals are old-fashioned or no longer apply. We must stand on the Word and believe the promises that are associated with them. Standing will take effort. You will need to avoid distractions that seek to throw you off balance and trip you up. At times, your own foundation will not be enough. You will need the support of the Holy Spirit and the Word of God to remain in position.

Ephesians 6:13-14 states, "Wherefore take unto you the whole armor of God, that ye may be able to withstand in the evil day, and having done all, to stand. Stand therefore, having your loins girt about with truth, and having on the breastplate of righteousness."

The truth is you will not be tempted beyond what you are capable of resisting. Fill yourself with the word of truth, the righteousness that comes through your surrender to Jesus Christ and stand. You may need support (walker), you may need balance (hold on to God's hand), but do not deter from the posture and position of obedience. God rewards, finds favor with, and is pleased by our obedience. 2 Chronicles 16:9— "For the eyes of the Lord run to and fro throughout the whole earth, to show Himself strong on behalf of those whose heart is loyal to Him." God is looking for someone to bless because of their loyalty and obedience. Will it be you? Remember, only what you do for Christ will last. "Therefore, my beloved brothers, be steadfast, immovable, always abounding in the work of the Lord, knowing that in the Lord your labor is not in vain" (I Corinthians 15:58 says, ESV).

LaKesha L. Williams Bio

LaKesha L. Williams, acclaimed author, speaker, and minister of the Gospel of Jesus Christ was born to parents Doris & Cleo Williams in Raleigh, North Carolina in 1983. To know LaKesha is to experience a calming spirit infused with gut-wrenching laughter at unexpected times. She has a passion for giving, which is demonstrated wholeheartedly through her founding of Born Overcomers Inc. a need based nonprofit organization & movement dedicated to promoting the belief that we were all Born to Overcome!

She has authored eleven books; including three bestsellers; and is also a featured co-author in *Open Your G.I.F.T.S.* presented by actress & comedian Kim Coles. She is the Owner and Lead Visionary of the Vision to Fruition Group LLC, a consulting firm dedicated to helping others bring their visions to fruition. In 2015, LaKesha received the *Sista's Inspiring Sista's Phenomenal Woman Award*, since she has gone on to become the 2016 Indie Author Legacy Award Recipient in the Author on the Rise category, a *2016 Metro Phenomenal Woman Honoree*, a *2017 TDK Publishing Author of the Year* nominee & the *2018 iShine Awards* winner for *Author of the Year*. LaKesha is currently a student at Capital Bible Seminary pursuing a master's degree in Christian Care.

LaKesha, as a virgin herself, is also an advocate of abstinence, purity, and virginity until marriage. Currently, LaKesha resides in Maryland and enjoys serving in the community, fellowshipping with her church family at The Remnant of Hope International Church in Prince Frederick Maryland under the leadership of Pastor Margo Gross and spending time with her family and friends watching movies, sharing stories and creating new memories.

Contact Info.

Web: www.vision-fruition.com

www.bornovercomers.com

www.thehustleplanner.com

www.coachkesha.com

Cell#: 240-343-3563

Facebook Pages:

Born Overcomers Inc.

The Vision to Fruition Group

The Hustle Planner

Coach Kesha

Personal Facebook: www.facebook.com/lakesha.williams

Twitter & Instagram: @iamcoachkesha

Run Like Hell!

"I am worth the fight. I am hope personified."

by Rashieda Addison

Run Like Hell!

By Rashieda D. Addison

I ran like hell. I leapt over the fence with a flawless stride. I don't recall pausing to cross the street as my mommy emphatically taught me. I did not look both ways. I could only see the safety on the other side of our one-bedroom basement apartment door—the lower-level penthouse of a four-family flat, all brick. This downstairs dungeon was my deliverance from him. A living room. A bedroom for my brothers and I made up of twin bunk beds. A bathroom and further down an open space just before the kitchen are where my mom and intermittently present stepfather slept. I remember he killed a mouse with a dustpan as we enjoyed King-Vitamin cereal. I think Focus Hope's generic version of Captain Crunch. I loved it, nevertheless. The mouse tried to run like hell but had no chance. These daily activities did not interrupt the swinging of my happy breakfast legs at the kitchen table that was also part of their bedroom decor.

He used to use me to satisfy his desires like dry humping. I am not sure if he was abused and so he abused me. He would touch me and hump on me every chance he got. Let me be clear, the use of "every" does not necessarily mean many especially since I can only recall a few times. I was young and time recall lags. Kenneth was the eldest son of the family across the street who lived in a single-family home. Maybe it was a two-family flat. In hindsight, they must have been well to do. He was dumb-literally. At any rate, I recall them coming over for basement parties. It was the after party that I looked forward to. For my baby brother, a stroll around the table to enjoy leftover alcohol and for me the skewered hotdog, pickle, government cheese chunk hors d'oeuvres. Poor baby brother found himself inebriated, constipated, and toppled onto the bathroom floor. I was terrified. His head bump caused a little cut. All I saw was blood. "Maaaaaaaaaaa! Mamaaaaa! Ma!" I yelled. She came running, amused by what she discovered and saved the day.

Back to that unsavory day in Detroit. Wearing my pink polyester shorts and matching flowered turtleneck t-shirt, I answered Kenneth's phone call telling me, "Come over here." I was hesitant but I complied.

I took a jay-walk across 16th Street and to the backdoor to enter their home. One step into the kitchen and was summoned to the bedroom. A kid luring a kid. There he stood at the head of the bed with his pants at his ankles. Holding his shirt over himself. Attempting to be shy and modest about a premeditated plan that began with the directive, "Take down your shorts." I stood at the foot of the bed, shorter than the footboard, like a deer in headlights. Starring. Frozen. I cased the joint like the Equalizer, looking back at the door gauging how long it would take me to turn around and run out the door. Simultaneously, hoping to get caught, but not get caught taking part in his mischief. Afterall, I ran my "fast-tail" across the street without permission. I felt guilty.

"C'mon on take your shorts off!" he requested again. I looked at him, and I could see a part of him that at the age of five I should not have been exposed to. It was unrighteous to my eyes. It was no longer covered by his shirt. He was preparing to, "stick me up." After a third request, I acted as if I had lowered my shorts with an up down motion. He told me to come get on the bed and began to walk toward me. I could see a part of him that I cannot erase from my brain. It was both a blessing and curse. The sight of him provoked a fear in me that gave me the courage to navigate the corners of the home without hesitation. Turn, step, step, left, table bump, door, screen door, don't look back. I ran down the stairs, to the gate, up and over in a single bound and down the side pathway into the street, missing any cars that had just passed by or were too slow to meet me at that designated place in time. I made it to the haven of home, the one-bedroom basement apartment that saved me from a 14-year old's desire to rob me. "Ye did run well; who did hinder you that ye should not obey the truth" (Galatians 5:7)?

I wonder what Sporty would have done to him if he had known. I wonder if he would have protected me like he protected his reputation.

141134

They say we marry our fathers. Well, I married my father and stepfather. No matter the circumstance, role models, especially father figures, train girls on how to deal with men. My stepdad, a masterful street mechanic, disconnected my phone call, to force me to talk to him. We had a push button phone that could be carried around the house with the aid of an extended extension cord. With the pressure of the pointer finger, both buttons would retract, and the phone call would successfully cease. As a teenager, I thought this was grounds for copping a legitimate attitude with a dude who was inebriated and crushed about not being his baby girl's biological father. His beef was with my mother and probably himself. I said it with a stare that meant, "You are not my daddy so don't start acting like it." My mother was my boss and in the back of my mind "my real daddy" would be home one day to replace him. My squinted eyes warned him, "Please know that I am not going to 'tell on you' for hanging up the phone on my boyfriend to ask me who I thought my daddy was." My answer, articulated with the shifting of my lips to the left, spoke for the first time, undoubtedly, "My daddy is Sporty."

"Tell Sporty to come back." said the man whose dog my dad had killed for attacking him. Some day in 1974, while I was fresh out of the warmth of my mother's womb, my father answered the call. I often questioned, "How could he put this man, his ego and his big bad reputation before his baby girl?" He went back to the man's house and after the dust settled, the dog owner died from the stab wound not viewed as self-defense. Dad ended up absent from the scene of the crime and in the hospital, with forever embedded shotgun pellets in his shoulder blade. One reason I had to touch my father. A memorable visit exploring the details consumed our conversation. I was full of questions, pauses and sighs that were laced with the theme, "What about me?"

Despite barely knowing him, Sporty was my hero. The man that my brothers teased me about amidst boyish chuckles and the profane words, "Your daddy is a jailbird!" In my mind, a fantasy and faith filled place, my knight in white shining armor was coming home one day to rescue me from life as I knew it. I held tightly to the story my grandma told me about him leaving a whopping three-hundred dollars with my mom prior to him going to what would be his final resting place. Inmate number 141134. Leaving the money was a noble deed. But the abandonment.

Ouch. I welcomed any reason to believe that he cared about me and like most inner-city kids, my daddy would come home one day. I had been looking for him. Longing for him. Hoping that he would show up like a military dad returning from being deployed overseas.

The Easter of my 12th year I wore a purple and white flowery dress to visit him. It was a transitional dress from little girls to little ladies. We sat on the picnic tables during the visit. Despite the entertainment of a prisoner and his female visitor sneaking intimate feels under the picnic table, my daddy was of priority. I was fresh off punishment that included being collared by my mom. I closed my door and she thought I slammed it. In my feelings, I was missing something that I never had. He left when I was two months old. I could not wait to turn eighteen when I could visit him without an escort. For forty-two years and ten months of my life, he remained incarcerated. A natural life prison sentence was realized, followed by an unnatural death, Hepatitis C, and liver disease. Sporty didn't make my 5th grade promotion for my rendition of *The Greatest Love of All*, my high school graduation speech, college graduation for my heel kick, so I was hoping he'd make it to his grandson's college graduation in three years. My longing for him, lay dormant inside me.

On December 20, 1997, I graduated from college. On that same day, I met my first husband. On December 20, 2000, I gave birth to our son. He was conceived in love among two friends with too many issues to name. On December 21, 2010, I was granted a divorce. In 1997, my ex-husband, seven years older than I, had recently obtained freedom. He avoided liver disease but suffered from post-incarceration syndrome. He was tall, dark, and handsome. I was fresh out of college. He was a very well preserved 30-year-old. I was a 23-year-old girl unaware of what lay dormant inside of me.

I met him at a nightclub hours after my graduation turn-up in the church's basement. As we danced, the small of his back and placement of his hands sucked me in. He sealed the deal with conversation about going to church at 7 a.m. He asked me to go home with him. I gently touched his face and assured him that that was not what he wanted from me. Days later, I fell for the banana in the tailpipe trick.

Inseparable, we laughed, partied, and struggled together. We went to church together to fix all that ailed us but to no avail. He served another two-year bit. We were a year into being a family until the day we pulled up to my home in two separate cars. A van backed into our driveway. I was terrified as he jumped out of the car to approach the van. I begged him to get back into his car. I called the police. They arrived quickly but not soon enough to catch the van as it pulled off in haste with the wrong license plate. I was not sure if the van was there for him, to break into our home or the neighbors place but I was terrified. I was violated and unprotected. The last iota of trust was gone. Not long after separating and moving home with my mother, back to the same neighborhood I had escaped, I ran like hell. His story is not mine to tell but it was a tumultuous relationship filled with absenteeism and recidivism that left my son and I, fatherless.

Father to the Fatherless

With my six-year-old son in tow, I moved over five hundred miles to the east coast with a television in my backseat and nowhere to live. I had to go. I knew that I would not be able to reject him for I longed for his presence just as much as he longed to be present. So, I ran like hell. Within a two-week time, frame, I interviewed, packed, and moved to Maryland.

Ironically, my son and I lived with my ex's family member for a month until we secured a place to call home. Later I signed up for therapist number one for my son and number four for myself. This was after my son, with tears in his eyes, questioned why I could not just be with his dad. The waterworks flowed and the feelings of hopelessness ran strong and deep. I called my mom, five hundred miles away, she could get a prayer through.

Praise be to God for my mother who decided to make her call and election sure. This monumental step in her life changed the trajectory of her children's lives. Her story is her story to tell, but as she sat in the courtroom watching her second baby's dad be sentenced to natural life imprisonment, I am sure she felt hopeless. There goes baby daddy number two. I often imagined people looking at the two-month-old baby girl in her arms envisioning a bleak and hopeless future. Extended family members discussed the situation and shook their heads with thoughts of hopelessness coupled with no plans to help the fatherless little girl. Psalm 68:5 says, "Father of the fatherless and protector of widows, is God in his holy habitation." He who numbers the hairs on our head will certainly not turn away from the children living as orphans, and this should inspire us to act.

Unapologetically Me

I have successfully met many stereotypical quotas due to absent fathers. I diligently looked for love in all the right wrong places. I lacked knowledge of self and self-worth—the product of being a black girl in America with few positive images of herself. I was taught that it is better to marry than burn. I had little direction on choosing a mate. I married twice for asinine reasons. I guess this speaks to why I have been serviced by six individual therapists. The church house has been my haven and holding steady at therapist number seven. Raised with a strong apostolic background, I obtained a foundation full of good old fire and brimstone teaching. I interpreted some things incorrectly and have worked to debunk those things along with other dogmas.

My second husband did not like the church I chose as home and eventually the church folded. Abandoned, I lingered for over a year with no covering. I needed a church home. I simply wanted a church where the pastor knew my child's name. My first time showing up to The Remnant of Hope International Church, the pastor said, "How is Daniel?" I was shocked that she remembered my son's name. It meant the world to me. That was the final confirmation that I had found a church home. The first confirmation was when I had walked into service, Pastor was at the podium in full stride. Not long after my tardy behind sat down, she began to cry out with a trembling voice and tears in her eyes. "Sis, he is not the one! He is not the one," she repeated and repeated. I looked around, with the internal question, "Is she talking to me?" I totally answered with self-assurance, "She is *not* talking to me." Looking straight ahead, I did not flinch, no sudden moves. I saw another sister crying her eyes out. Oh, she is talking to her. I think. Could she be prophetically talking about the man that was living with me? The man that would weeks later put his hands on me. The man that my son would bum rush to the bed to protect me from his nasty tone. The man I would have to file a personal protection order against for a year? The man who would have to be escorted to my home to retrieve his life from the closet downstairs. He was still aggressive with the policeman present. "Officer please tell him not to talk to me." I asked. Yup, he was not the one, but this was the shepherd I was looking for! A clear conduit for me, transparent and humane.

I have found a seat of solace, peace, rest, liberty to worship God, serve his people and to be authentic self. I sing and I can't, I laugh and joke, I love call and response, I give great hugs on purpose and I talk about wanting dating, marriage, and sex without judgmental side-eyes. I mean, the church is supposed to be a non-judgmental place. Within the church, my truth should be on a metaphoric mantle with a label. Like in a laboratory with jars of extracted "broken hearts, smoke-filled livers and alcohol enlarged kidneys." I am healing. Medicated with a prognosis of a long road of looking to fill the gaps created by a distant daddy. Daily, I take a dose of fighting to love myself inside and out. I live my life out loud. Transparent to a fault. Fighting falling prey to the creepy thoughts that crawl through my ears, eyes and into my brain. I choose to share and expose my truth. Hiding truth serves as landmines for those creepy crawlers creating the battlefield in my mind. Some people are uncomfortable with my approach to sanity. I am a contradiction to perceived me. I know that, *"There's nothing enlightened about shrinking so that others won't feel insecure or uncomfortable around you."* –Marianne Williamson, *Our Deepest Fear.*

I have been in many church services broken mentally, emotionally, physically, and financially. Embarrassed by it all. Leaving the way, I came. Not that anyone knew but as Langston Hughes' Luella Bates Washington Jones said, "I wouldn't tell God if he didn't already know." But what I have told God, "Yo, I am sorry. I am effed up. I ain't got much of nothing except this joy and this worship. From there, dirty brown teardrops create roadmaps of my pain. A bellowed scream, the sound of an alarm, I have been doing this too long. There is an urgency, a request right now, God. The nose teardrops as salty as the Dead sea. I fade to black and nothing really matters at all, because in this moment, for my God, desperately, for my enlightenment and sanity, I am unapologetically me.

I smile often. Gap fully exposed. Thereafter, I walk tall and I remix my reality from places of sorrow, struggle, and lack by having faith in my faith and internalizing the fact: the joy of the Lord is my strength! I continue to live my best life despite my past, present, not having enough, my mistakes and my choices. It is a fight, a mental struggle and conscious process. I am worth the fight. My lineage is worth the fight. You who are reading this are worth the fight. I continue to show up as the fearless, fatherless daughter, promising, promiscuous teen, and whole broken adult. I am hope personified.

I know of many stories about abuse. I have a few of my own. How the abused become abusers, drug addicts, prostitutes, or inmates. I could have a myriad of titles given the scenario of my reality at two months old. But who would have predicted my today? The book of Jeremiah, 8:11 states, "For I know the plans I have for you," declares the Lord, "plans to prosper you and not to harm you, plans to give you hope and a future." As of late, some of us at church have coined a phrase that is the witness of something mind blowing, overwhelming, unreal, and only accountable to the omnipotent, omniscient, and omnipresent might of God. And so, I leave you with that phrase:

MY GOD, TODAY!

Pastor Margo's Heap of Hope

Wholeness, the state of being well in mind, body, and spirit is God's desire for his children. He wants us whole. Not in broken pieces with our hearts in one place, our mind in another, and our spirits trapped in our pain. God wants us whole. Many of us walk around with holes where love should be, where peace should live, and where the security that comes from our father should live. These holes must be filled. Some of us try to fill the void with quick counterfeits. These fake versions take up spaces they were never meant to fill only to leave us more broken than before. If we are not careful, our quick attempts at patch work will result in cycles of bitterness, self-hate, and distrust. But God has everything we need to fill the void. It does not matter what that void is or who the void represents. If you need it, God's got it. You will find God to be the water for your thirst, your advocate when you have no support, and your father when you feel abandoned.

When Jesus met the man at the pool of Bethesda, he asked him one simple question, "Do you want to be made whole." This question reveals two things; 1. Your desire for wholeness matters and 2. You can be made whole even if life made you broken. Jesus is asking that of you today. Do you have the desire to live in wholeness? Even if you have never known the feeling of completeness in God. He is able, willing, and will make you whole. The impotent man's answer reveals something I have found to be true. We often get fixated on the how instead of the result. The man responds with the reason he is not whole. He explains that there is no one to put him in the pool. This man limited God's ability to make him whole to one source, the pool. God is a great big God who has multiple ways of carrying out the same task. Jesus is standing before the man, but the man is looking at the pool. What excuse have you given God? He is standing at the ready to make you whole. Do not blame the pool when you're standing before power. Jesus was the power. Jesus was only concerned about the desire, not the method. He was the way and is the way today. He is the way to wholeness. Cry out to God today. Cry, "I want to be made whole." Then rest in faith that he is making you just that. Expect the removal of the counterfeits to make room for the real thing.

The Bio of Rashieda D. Addison, B.A., MSCIA

Rashieda D. Addison was raised by her mother Kathy Addison-Henderson and is the second eldest of four children, Donald, Maurice, and Samantha. Rashieda holds a bachelor's degree in Secondary Education-English and a master's degree in Curriculum, Instruction and Assessment. She began her career in her hometown Detroit, Michigan prior to relocating to Maryland. 40 years ago, Rashieda joined the Rose of Sharon COGIC and has a lifetime membership.

Currently, Rashieda serves as an assistant principal and adjunct faculty member in the DMV.

Rashieda is the proud mother of Daniel, a college student-athlete and they are members of The Remnant of Hope International Church. She honors her mother and father, George Meyers, Jr. as great teachers of life lessons such as, "Seek to give unconditional love, spirit knows spirit and everything that comes up does not have to come out!"

Rashieda lives by the scripture, Nehemiah 8:10 "...for the JOY of the LORD is your strength!"

Contact Info.

Web: https://bit.ly/rashiedaaddison

Dominion Over the Darkness

"Darkness as I experienced it only produced fruit no one wanted."

by Alkeisha Williams

Dominion Over the Darkness

by Alkeisha Williams

"Who Are You?"

Who are you? Who-who, who-who?

I really want to know.

-Lyrics by The Who (1978)

Birth to 13 years

One or two small toys, the first mail I ever received. No idea who/what "From Your FATHER" is supposed to mean to me. But I love gifts, and I am grateful for anything I get. I will even play with the box it's in—there is no end to fun I imagine making little much. Yet no sensory details conjured—sight, sound, smell, touch, taste—all fail to bring you to mind, yet I am conscious of you. Five witnesses and none of them prove your existence beyond a reasonable doubt!

How? Wait, scramble that. Who? Who are you?

Mommy said I was the "queen of questions", so you know I asked, right? Faithful to task, so sorry you were not. Fidelity fleeting, you moved on. And still, her answer to my inquiry did not paint you in a negative light. —Man, that girl is good! —But they sure were wide brush strokes with lack luster color and abstractions.

I am too young for this. I cannot make out what this is supposed to be.

Shapeless. SHIFTLESS. Line, depth, foreground, background—all angles. NOTHING. Clueless, art - but only to the extent that it is a "reflection" of my reality. Commentary that says much but communicates nothing, contributes nothing...meaningful, that is.

So, I lie in bed with my questions wondering—Who are you?

Mommy saw my math and hurt for me. My subtraction took something from her—or she was already missing something, and you took more. I am not sure. It is a variable I'll never really solve for. Either way, she taught me multiplication instead and tried to love me twice as much. Sometimes I don't think she kept any for herself, though. But the division was ever present, even if you were not. How can my "0" be rational? Just because you write it in many forms. So?!

And why isn't it considered prime when it feels important to me; don't talk to me about divisors. I don't really care what distracted you, took you away, caused you to split our fact family. You traded it for another. That's what I heard, but it doesn't change my remainder, zero.

On one point I agree. It is complex and real, and raw. Now, that's some data for you with a downward trend if you look closely enough. God, help me. I'm at a loss. Who are you?

"Waiting on You"

I don't mind waiting, don't mind waiting

Don't mind waiting on you"

-Lyrics by Juanita Bynum (2006)

Age 14-18 years

Me: Hello?

Caller: Hello, is this Alkeisha?

Me: Yes, this is she (mommy taught me well).

Caller: Uhhh, hi baby. This is your father.

Me: Who?

Caller: Your father, Michael. Now, I know I haven't been there, but I'd like for us to talk.

Me: My father?

Caller: Yeah, can I pick you up?

Me: Ummmmm, I don't know. I guess so. I have to be at work by 2:00pm.

Caller: Alright, I'll pick you up. I can drop you there.

Me: Uhhh, ok.

He arrived at the house at 1:30p in an old black Batmobile with red interior. I glanced at him, nervous, hopeful, overwhelmed at the sight of him. He was 6-feet tall and handsome. Mocha brown skin. "Who are you?" I thought to myself. He reminded me of a movie star—a combination of Billy D. Williams and Laurence Fishburne. And I related to him the same way that day. In awe but walking away not really knowing who this man was any more than I did the one on the cover of that VHS tape. Was it a cover? What was he up to? Why now? Why here? After all this time? I'm working, for God's sake! My father?! Nah, can't be. But I do kind of look like him. "Girl, you don't know this dude," a voice kept screaming in my head. Of course, I had my escape plan. I slid as close as I could to the passenger door and waited to see if he would lock it. He didn't, but if he had, my mind was so gone I think I would have hurt him. He spoke in low masculine terms that I had never heard before and didn't really know what to do with. He carried the conversation (highly abnormal if you know me). I don't remember ANYTHING he said to me that day. The only thing I shared was the address of where we were headed. To tell the truth, I wanted nothing more than to blink and be there already. A 15-minute trip felt like an eternity. I was soooo uncomfortable that I could not wait to get out. "My shift starts at 2:00 p.m. Sorry." I mumbled as I dashed from the car into my job.

After a week or so, he said he wanted to pick me up so we could get to know each other and talk more. An anxious excitement crept up in me. "He wants to get to know me." Days passed and the big day came. I was ready at 8:00 a.m. as agreed. Mom always told me to be early on-time and never have people waiting for you. So, at 7:00 a.m. I was fully dressed, hair done, wrapped in my coat, hat, and gloves, and seated on the couch in the living room. Every 10 minutes, I sprang from my seat to look out each window in search of hope. 7:00 a.m. turned into 8:00 a.m. and 8:00 a.m. into 9:00 a.m. with no sign of him. I called the number he gave me. No answer. "Sit down. He'll be here soon," I tried telling myself in vain. The hours waxed on, but I could not bring myself to do anything different but sit there.

This would become a familiar scene on and off for years until the hope I had of building anything faded. A dim, distant image of what should be. What are we doing here? Inevitably, it would end with my finally talking to him by phone that night or within a few days only to hear him say, "Oh, it must have slipped my mind." New promise to make it up to me. Old scene conjured again and again. When I did see him, he felt the need to give advice about my choices, my college, my major, my future career. "Computers are the way to go," he would say. He was very opinionated. I didn't really care about that stuff. But what I did care about I don't think he cared about—ME; The real me.

"Missing Me"

Loving you has thrown me

Loving you is lonely

Loving you is lonely

You better be missing me

-Lyrics by Angela McMahon

Ages 21-39

I thought attendance was a quantifiable measure. I guess it's because the numbers did not add up for me. How can you be present and absent at the same time? Sure, over the next several years I met a few people from the family. They were nice enough. Some I could take or leave because I could tell it was all a show (although I am not sure for who because I wasn't entertained). Either way, one would think that with all this new "family," I would feel warm and welcomed, I would feel like I belonged. In actuality, the opposite was true. I still could not say that I knew him or them. I never really got to know the people I met (other than my sisters, my uncle, and stepmother). I accepted that I was rejected. A second thought. Or worse, an afterthought—the black sheep. And my black was not beautiful. It was dark and deep. Like the pit I found myself in wrestling with my thoughts and questions. There was a popular quotation that floated through the air at my HBCU: "The darker the berry, the better the fruit." I know I should have felt a sense of black pride in the statement, but my twisted thinking did not....and not just because I'm light skinned. Dark-ness as I experienced it only produced fruit no one wanted. It consumed my thoughts, ugly, debasing, unraveling, awful thoughts from which questions sprang that plagued me still from my childhood to this prime time.

I looked for love in all the wrong places from people who could not give me what I needed anyway on their best day. I met a man who was different than anyone I had hooked up with before. It is a long, complicated story, but we eventually married and had a son together. For all the joy they brought, I still was not healed. For years, I wept at the altar in public and in private as my unworthiness tended to resurface in God's presence. God called me to be a worship leader, and I cannot tell you how many times I feel I left the people as I sobbed through my struggle and still sought to serve Him. I would ask Him how I was supposed to encourage other people when I don't even feel encouraged. I poured over His Word, read books, and begged God to deliver me from me. I experienced short-lived seasons of success but no lasting victory. And then, the unthinkable happened.

In the year 2000 after begging God for seven years for another child, I got pregnant. I was so grateful to God for hearing my prayer and for answering my heart's cry. My son would have another sibling. My husband would have another child. Honestly, boy or girl, it didn't matter. Both of us were just elated that it finally happened. As most expectant mothers do, I told everybody. We made calls to our parents and extended family to share the good news. It would not be long before we gave the good news to folks at church and in our community. Some had even been standing with me in faith for another child. We were all beside ourselves with excitement. I discovered it early within the first 2-3 weeks. But a month or so later, I began cramping and spotting. The doctor said there was nothing he could do. It was a waiting game. My faith said continue to stand. God would not have given you a baby if He did not plan to take it to term. He is the giver and sustainer of all life. I prayed. I worshipped. But after close to 3 months, I lost the baby. Pardon me for the graphic nature of what I am about to share, but the image is burned into my memory.

I was alone. My husband had to work because he had taken off so much to take me to prior appointments. Secretly, I resented him for not being with me. I needed him. But I understood. I had the urge to use the restroom, but when I got up, I could feel something was wrong. When I made my way to the commode, I heard it. I passed the baby right there, barely recognizable. Blood everywhere. I instantly lost it, fell to the floor, and laid there feeling dizzy, nauseated, and completely overwhelmed by the weight of what seemed like a ton of bricks. Confused, disillusioned, I cried until I could not cry any more. It did not make sense. My faith was shaken undeniably. What in the world was going on? "If you forsake me, where can I go?" I lamented. Why would you do this? Why me? Why? Why? Why? The answers to my questions never came. But I do know He heard them. Time is a blur after that. I had sunk into the deepest pit I had ever seen. I went numb. It was hard to feel anything, like it was unreal. I cried myself to sleep most nights. All my husband could do was pray for me, hold me, and rock me to sleep. I did not want to see anyone. I did not want to talk to anyone. I do not know if I ever gave my husband the grace and space to mourn the loss. I could not help it. I was devastated. What I did not know was that my husband had my immediate circle of friends all praying for me. He was concerned about me. When I came to myself and had a notion to go to church, it was all I could do to get out of the bed. This will sound strange, but I am not exaggerating. God talked me through every detail of that morning: taking a shower, brushing my teeth, getting dressed. Everything! I must have been on the verge of a nervous breakdown. When I got to service, I just stood there. I did not lead worship with the team as I normally would have. I couldn't even if I tried. The worship was high; and I knew it, but I couldn't feel anything.

I clearly remember one date night years ago when my husband and I sat and watched the movie *The Secret Life of Bees* based on the book by Sue Monk Kidd. The movie, set in South Carolina in 1964, tells of a teenage white girl named Lily who struggles with the loss of her mother and harsh discipline of an abusive father. After fleeing her father and living with the Boatwright women for some time, Lily has a heart to heart talk with the eldest sister and breaks down in tears. Falling to her knees, she exclaims, "I'm unlovable!" At that, I gasped aloud and burst into tears as I ran from the room and locked myself in the bathroom. What ensued was the ugliest cry I think I had ever had at that point. It was as if Lily screamed the words of my own heart. She voiced the pain I carried daily but never resolved. I was probably there on the floor of our bathroom for about an hour rocking and moaning: "I need you, God! Help me! Hold me! Please!!! I don't think I can take this!"

The work of finding freedom required much from me and yet gave me what I needed the most. I was a grown woman, married with a family, and still wrestled with depression and low self-esteem. It would take years, but one step at a time, little by little God would walk me through the healing process. He taught me first and simply that He loved me just the way I was, BEFORE I ever felt differently, thought differently, behaved differently. He loved me. Jeremiah 31:3 (AMP) records, "I have loved you with an everlasting love; Therefore, with lovingkindness I have drawn you and continued My faithfulness to you." If others did not, He did. Not only that but He told me that He chose me. ME? Huh? This radical truth wrecked me. At that time, I felt cast away, abandoned, less than, far from CHOSEN! He says in John 15:16a (AMP), "You have not chosen Me, but I have chosen you and I have appointed and placed and purposefully planted you, so that you would go and bear fruit and keep on bearing, and that your fruit will remain and be lasting." Wow! This was rich. Father, if You love me and chose me, free me from this heaviness. It's unbearable. I feel like I can't breathe, like something is holding me under water and I'm drowning. He whispers 2 Timothy 1:7 (AMP), "For God did not give us a spirit of timidity or cowardice or fear, but [He has given us a spirit] of power and of love and of sound judgment and personal discipline [abilities that result in a calm, well-balanced mind and self-control]." I held those truths to be self-evident and declared my independence from anxiety, fear, depression, and low self-esteem. I wish I could tell you it was a "one and done" situation, but I can't. It would be years before I renewed my mind to a point that resembled good health.

I grew from there to learn practical ways to combat depression, to keep my hard-fought freedom. I asked God in prayer for an early warning system where there would be an alert or set of procedures in place indicating an impending emergency or potential problem. I asked that the Holy Spirit set off my inner alarm system when I started slipping back into that old familiar place. True to who He is, He has done just that.

"Remnants"

Your Justice sustains me,

Your life fulfills me, Oh God.

I am the remnant of the chosen one.

We are the remnants of the chosen ones.

-Lyrics by Elizondo, Mora, et.al. (2013)

Age 40-Present

Neither my problem nor my process came without a PROMISE! God is a promise maker and a promise keeper. As a matter of fact, looking back, I can see that He gave me a personal promise and promise for what He would do through me for others. Although I didn't know what it would look like or what the details would be, God promised that 1) the "Depths of darkness and depression you have seen will pale in comparison to the heights of joy you will experience in Me." and 2) I "would teach and admonish others how to get into His presence." At the time, if you had asked me if any good could come from the pain and frustration I was experiencing, I would have dismissed it. I could not conceive how God could use the darkness, use the torment, use the confusion and the chaos to grow me or help someone else. Well, He did and continues to do so. His Word consistently sustains me. When I am weak, He is strong in me. When I come to the end of myself, I find Him with open arms and strength unwavering.

Today, after a season of transition in nearly every area of my life, I am walking out the word He spoke to me 20 years ago! God planted me in good ground at The Remnant of Hope International Church, gave me community with other like-minded believers and covered me with an unconventional, preaching powerhouse in Pastor Margo Gross. By His grace, I am teaching and admonishing others how to get into His presence weekly! What a wonder! It gives me such joy to serve God and His people. I am honored to lift the One whose love lifted me. I am humbled to bless the One who blessed me! I am compelled to praise the Promise Maker and the Promise Keeper! He's ALL my help, all my hope, all my strength! I can testify to the truth: He is a Way Maker, Miracle Worker, Promise Keeper, Light in the Darkness—My God, that is who You are!!!

So, before you allow the circumstances of your birth to define your identity, please heed the truth. No matter how you got here—incest, rape, abusive marriage, out of wedlock, or whatever—God loves you with a love that will NEVER end, with a love that will NEVER fail, with a love that will never run out on you. Before your thoughts cause you to question your very existence, lay hold of this. Each one of us that graces the earth has a distinct purpose in God's plan. Celebrate the fact that YOU are HERE, and God is committed to using your story to bless others. He is so omnipotent and omniscient, so absolutely incredible, that He can use the dark places of your life to bring LIGHT and LIFE to the world. He can use what embarrassed, discouraged, and injured you to bring ENCOURAGEMENT, HEALING and WHOLENESS to someone else. He can use what almost took you out to be a LIFELINE of rescue to all who see and hear. Trust Him; He never fails.

Pastor Margo's Heap of Hope

The perfect storm is used to describe the presence of a combination of phenomena that result in a perfect situation for a storm to occur. The irony is that most of us do not like storms and do not see anything perfect about them. Consider this, storms uproot and expose anything that is not stable. It takes high winds, pressure, and flooding to reveal what was never rooted. It is not in the good moments that we know what is meant to remain with us, it is in the storm. The storms shake up our lives and remove things and people that are not sure. That tree that you thought would always be there may be found flat with exposed roots. It looked secure; the storm exposed that it was not. That is what the storms of life do. They force us to consider if our lives are as stable as we had hoped.

Here is the good news! What remains after the storm is rooted, dependable, tested and tried. Look around you! What made it to the other side. Not just the materialistic things. Don't just consider the people who remained. What about you? Are you here? Did you make it through? Did you survive the storm? You did because your roots held you. The Lord kept you. The Bible tells us when we don't walk in the counsel of the ungodly nor standeth in the way of sinners, nor sitteth in the seat of the scornful we will be like a tree planted (Psalm 1:1-3). It shows the tree is planted by rivers of water. This means it is near the source of its provision. In addition, the tree brings forth fruit in season, doesn't wither, and whatever he does prospers.

Storms will come and storms will go. Winds will blow and rain will fall, but you are planted. You made it through some unbelievable storms. You are still here. Rejoice that you are still planted, rooted, and bringing forth fruit. You shall prosper, in Jesus' name.

Alkeisha Williams Bio

Alkeisha Williams, known affectionately as Keisha, is a Washington, DC Metro native. In addition to serving in the field of education, Keisha is known for her passionate worship and active leadership in music ministry for the last two decades in the household of faith. Delivered from a poverty mindset and profound depression, Keisha credits God's love for pulling her out of the pit! It is no wonder the Lord has called her to inspire and uplift others. Keisha can be quoted saying, "At my core, I am a lover of God and a lover of people. It's my desire to see all encounter Him in worship." Her most recent accomplishment was the birth of Alkeisha Williams Enterprises or A.W.E. Her vision is to "equip people of all nations to exercise their gifts and experience the presence and power of God in worship" as she invites them to Stand in AWE of Him! (Psalm 33:8b)

Contact Info.

Web: https://bit.ly/alkeishawilliams

It's My Turn Now

"When I testify about God being a healer, it's personal to me now."

by Agnes Gross

It's My Turn Now by Agnes Gross

2019 turned out to be an incredibly challenging year for me. I watched God move in my life in a tremendous way. I have worked in the medical field most of my working career. Always taking care of others before taking care of me.

It's My Turn Now.

Your body will let you know when something is wrong. I can testify to the fact that God is a healer, I have seen evidence of that by God giving a blind man his sight back. I can testify to the fact that God is a deliverer. I have seen and heard demons talk through a man that was cast out. *It's My Turn Now.* In January 2019 I finally went to a doctor to find out what was going on with me because my right leg would give out, and I would tumble down to the ground. I had an abnormal gait, but I needed to talk with a doctor.

It's My Turn Now.

The doctor told me that she did not know what was wrong. She sent me to see a neurologist in Oxon Hill, Maryland. I told my doctor that I felt like I had a stroke. I could not lift my left arm in the air. I thought that it could have been back problems because of the way that I was dragging my left leg. The doctor had me do several exercises in his office. He told me that I did not have a stroke, nor did I have back problems. Meanwhile, I was falling three to four times a week. He ordered an (MRI) Magnetic Resonance Imaging of the body for me to have done. The results came back showing nothing. My doctor ordered another MRI—this time with contrast. The contrast medium enhances the image quality and allows the radiologist more accuracy and confidence in their diagnosis.

It's My Turn Now

June 12, 2019, the results came back showing that I had a tumor embedded in my spine. I did not want surgery. My doctor said that this must be removed at once. I was feeling a little apprehensive about the news; tears started falling down my face. It is because of what happened next that has me in awe of God. It was all in God's timing that things were done. While sitting in his office my doctor (unbeknownst to me) called another doctor who was a specialist and renowned neurosurgeon. God always gives His best.

June 19, 2019, I met my neurosurgeon at George Washington University Hospital, and he explained what procedure I was going to have done. The medical term is cervical spinal fusion. I would have to get a metal plate screwed into the bone in my neck. On June 26, 2019, with God in the forefront, my husband, Kenneth Gross, Sr., and my son, Glenwood Young both at my side; my mother, Clara Ijams, Pastor Margo Gross, sons: Linwood Young, Alvin Holland; and my Remnant of Hope Church family praying behind me, God did His thing. My surgery was successful. Thank you, Jesus, what a mighty God we serve. The tumor was benign—look at God!!! When I testify about God being a healer, it is personal to me now. I am so honored that God used me to show that healing is a process. I realize with just one slip of the surgeon's hand I could have been paralyzed. I Praise God for his extensive vision over my life.

A special thank you goes to: my husband, Kenneth Gross who had to take on the house duties and took such good care of me; my son, Glenwood Young, who kept everyone updated on what was going on with me; my son, Linwood Young, who traveled from New York to spend time with me; Pastor Margo Gross, and Elder Trina Thomas for picking me up from the hospital; Kenneth Gross, Jr., who prepared meals for me before leaving for vacation the next day; I thank my loved ones and friends for visits from my mom Clara Ijams, and cousins: Gloria Jones, Olivia Jones and Agnes Jones, Ana and Joe Taylor. Sherman and Maxine Ijams, Robin Foote, Vivian Davis, Shanique Adams, Roxanne Parker, VaShawne and Dawnesha Gross, Noah, Nia, Dekari, Zakaria Holland and Tavion. Vanessa Gantt thank you for taking the time out each week to send me encouraging cards. Prayer still works. I give God glory for my story.

Pastor Margo's Heap of Hope

In Jeremiah 8:22 the Lord asks a question, "Is there a balm in Gilead?" Gilead was known for producing perfumes and ointments that were believed to have healing qualities. However, with all that children of Israel had done, that ointment was not enough to heal the land. No doctor, concoction, or antidote was found among them. They needed something they could not produce. They needed a healing to overtake them and get to the root and heart of the issue. The true Balm in Gilead is Jesus himself. We are reminded in Isaiah 53:5 that he was wounded for our transgressions, bruised for our iniquities. The chastisement our peace was upon him; and with his stripes we are healed. Not we shall be healed, or we might be healed, but we ARE healed.

The bad report is just a report; our faith must remain in that balm. The balm that was activated years ago that we might walk in the fullness of our healing. The gospels are full of testimonies of healing. In most cases Jesus shows that "your faith has made you whole" (Mark 5:34, Mark 10:52, & Luke 17:19). Hold fast to your faith. Hang on. Healing is near. Healing is now. Receive it. Receive your soul's healing. Receive your heart's healing and yes, receive your physical healing. You are the beneficiary of Christ's sacrifice on Calvary. His will says that you inherit healing. Walk in it!

Agnes Gross Bio

Agnes Gross is a native of Calvert County, Maryland, born to Mrs. Clara Ijams and her stepdad, Mr. James Ijams who raised her. After graduating from Calvert High School, Agnes attended Charles County Community College for a year before passionately serving as a Geriatric Assistant for over 30 years. Those under Agnes' care absolutely adored her and saw her as family, understanding just how much she would do to help someone else in need.

Deeply committed to serving the Lord and His people, Agnes is a humble woman of God who will assure you that "only what you do for Christ will last," as she believes that God will get the glory out of her life. Even during the toughest time in her life when Agnes fell ill, she worshipped, praised, and thanked God fervently for surrounding her with a husband, children, family, church, and loved ones who prayed for and supported her. This time in her life assured Agnes that God is a healer and that healing is a process.

Agnes' passion for going to church is understated. In fact, there is no other place she would rather be as she is a faithful member of the Remnant of Hope International Church, under the leadership of her daughter-in-love, Pastor Margo M. Gross. Every Sunday Agnes can be found praising God and on Wednesday's, actively engaging in Bible Study lessons.

Agnes is a loving helpmate to the love of her life, Kenneth Gross, and together they remain in Calvert County Maryland, where most of her days are found listening to old-time gospel music and helping others in every way she possibly can. Agnes is the proud mother of her three children, stepmother of two stepsons, and the grandmother of ten, who love game night with the family. She is the ultimate competitor and a diehard New England Patriots fan who stands by her team to the end. Most importantly, everyone who is around Agnes, walks away feeling genuinely loved!

Contact Info.

Web: https://bit.ly/agnes-gross

God's Gotcha! Having Done All, Just Stand!

". . . if we are listening God always gives us a word to hold onto."

by Elbie Williams

God's Gotcha! Having Done All, Just Stand!

by Elbie Williams

People often question whether God is still doing miracles and is His Word true? Is this Jesus real? If He is, how do you know? Well, let us look at a few things He has done for me and you can decide for yourself.

The year is 2011. I have a son who has graduated from DeMatha High School and is a Freshman at Del State University, a wife who is an incredible English teacher in Calvert County, and I am a music teacher in the Washington, DC school system. I am having some significant health challenges (diabetes, high blood pressure, high cholesterol) and weight concerns after just completing an intense six-month weight loss program with my doctor who is trained and certified in bariatrics. My doctor and I decide to move forward with bariatric surgery. My wife and several of my family members did not agree with the decision, but they did not see the depression, self-hate, and embarrassment that came with being who I had become. I was now 355 lbs. I did not walk, I leaned from side to side as I tried to walk. Funny thing is I was still running full court basketball games, lifting weights, and pretending to be happy. I remember getting on a plane and having to use the seatbelt extension and that joint barely fit. What sealed my decision was going to Indiana University to celebrate 100 years of my fraternity and in the middle of posing for a picture, I fell on my knees and needed both of my line brothers to help me get up. After making sure I was ok of course they clowned me and I laughed and played it off, but I was really humiliated.

December 2011, surgery went well but it was very scary. Imagine waking up and not only are you in tremendous pain, there is a mask over your nose and mouth that is forcing oxygen in but because you aren't really fully aware of what is going on, you feel like you are suffocating. So, the thing that is supposed to be working for your good appears to be trying to take your life. It is totally dark in what is this huge room and there is no one in there with you or so it seems. All of a sudden you can hear footsteps coming close to you, you begin calling out but those footsteps fade because they can't hear you through the mask that covers your mouth. At first, I started to panic but then I began to remind myself that God got me, and I speak God's Word over myself. "He will never leave me nor forsake me!" "He is with me even to the ends of the earth." "He is my peace." "You got this big fella." Before I know it, I fall back to sleep.

The next time I wake up, I am in my room and my family (wife, sons, sister, parents) are standing around me. Well, everyone knew about my surgery except my oldest son. Because he was taking final exams, I told my wife not to tell him until he finished his exams. I could see the fear in his face. He had never seen me look so weak with tubes all over me. As I tried to reassure them that God had me, I quickly realized once again, they could not hear me because of the mask. I smiled and winked at them and they got it. All in all, everything went well. I healed a lot faster than others who had the same surgery. After getting through that first night of feeling alone, fearful and realizing no one could hear me, I felt like my faith was being tested. As a worship leader I often sing songs about Jesus being my help, my redeemer, and a mighty fortress, but I believe it's in the dark times and in our trials and tribulations that we see for ourselves whether the God we claim to serve is real. When I called on His name and spoke His Word, He heard me and delivered me from my fears.

June 2012 I am feeling good. I am about six months into recovery from surgery, I have lost about 50lbs but begin experiencing sharp pains in my sides. Of course, I ignore it. That is what I do because I have a high tolerance for pain. However, the pain gets worse. Immediately I start thinking it must be something going on from surgery, so I ask my wife to take me back to the hospital where I had surgery because they will know what to do. It takes about 45 minutes to get there and by this time I am in tears. Yes, I lost all my cool points. We sit in the packed waiting room for another 25 minutes. Finally, the nurse comes, we go to the back, and the testing begins. They do blood work, an MRI and give me medication to help with the pain. The doctor comes back and says, "There is nothing wrong with your surgery, everything looks great. You are passing kidney stones and we see about 7 or 8 more that will eventually come down." I say to him, "Thanks Doc." He replies, "There is something I am concerned about. You have two spots in your left kidney, and I need to get a biopsy done."

Now, I come from a family who have had our encounters with cancer and normally that is how the process begins. The biopsy—I do not sweat it, and we schedule an appointment to get it done. The doctor tells me it will only take about two days to get the results. Well, two weeks go by. Hey, you know the saying, "No news is good news." During church service several Sundays earlier, Pastor's title to his message was, "This is not as unto death" (John 11:4). The Word is always good, but I had no clue what was about to take place in my life. How many know if we are listening God ALWAYS gives us a word to hold on to. Sometimes it is for down the road and He will bring it back to remembrance. So, I go back for the follow-up and we are waiting in the doctor's office in the back for him to come in. 30 minutes go by and he walks in and says, "Hello. Yep it's cancer!" "It's in your upper and lower left kidney." To say the least, I was surprised at the way he just came in and put it out there without any warning whatsoever. Now remember earlier I said I come from a family who has had to deal with cancer for a long time. My father's dad and three of my dad's sisters died of cancer. My dad was healed of thyroid cancer. A few weeks before I was diagnosed, my cousin was also diagnosed with cancer. I am praying for her and now I have it. I asked the doctor what was next? The doctor gives me a few recommendations. He could do it or he could refer me to NIH. My dad went to NIH, so for me that was a no brainer. My wife and I leave the doctor's office and I am not ready to talk about it. She respects my wishes and we walk to the car. The truth is when the doctor told me I had cancer, I wanted to cry but I felt I needed to look like I was strong for my wife and family. My mind suddenly went back to all my family members who I had lost to this beast called cancer and my cousin who was dealing with it the same time I was. Finally, I am ready to talk, first my wife and I talk then the rest of our family. God reminds me of the word He gave me in John 11:4, "This sickness is not unto death but for the glory of God, that the Son of God may be glorified through it."

We set up the appointment with NIH. We meet the team of doctors. They explain the process and say they will take care of me for the rest of my life and it is free. This was a relief to know that this would not be a financial burden on my family. We now have my surgery date and God says to me, "You are healed." On my way to prep for surgery God says it again so I tell my wife. God said I am healed. We arrive at NIH, get prepped and I say to the Doctor. "You might want to check me first doc, I believe I am healed." He looks at me like I am crazy and sarcastically says, "Who told you that?" My reply, "My Jesus told me that, so you might want to check me out first." He again looks at me as if to say, "Yeah right Mr. Williams." And walks out. I go through surgery and I wake up. In pain, drugged up with that mask on again but this time I am cool collected and see my wife and doctor in the room. I hear the doctor ask, "Who told you that you had cancer in your upper and lower left kidney?" My wife and I both said, "You did. We saw the MRI picture." His response was, "There was only a small legion in your upper and we got all of it." In as much pain as I was in, I lifted both hands and began to worship in that place. I looked at the doctor and said, "I told you. I told you. God said I was healed!" The doctor had this puzzled look on his face and did not know what to say. This year makes eight years of being healed from cancer. God gave me a word and I believed only! Yes, there were times I was scared but every time scared attempted to become fear, I spoke God's Word over myself. God's gotcha!

August 2018, I am back teaching music in a charter school in Washington, DC. I had been away from teaching for about three years and I figure it is time to go back. I had left teaching in 2015, started my own lawn-care business and my barbering. Business was doing surprisingly good for a startup and it felt good being my own boss. The challenge I had was doing business with a company who at first did me well, but I started relying on this one company that ended up being my main source of income. Well, when that company pulled out on me it really had a negative impact on me financially. So, I learned as a business not to put all my eggs in one basket. Moving forward, I go back to teaching and it has changed in just three years, but I embrace it and do what I had done for 15 years—teach my students to have confidence, poise, respect, musicianship. The year starts off great. I am building relationships, building students, and being challenged as I get reacclimated to the classroom. While I am teaching and preparing my students for their winter concert, I start getting chest pains and pain shooting down my arm. Well, you know me. I ignore it and continue pressing on to getting my students ready. I am teaching grades pre-k through 8th grade, so you can imagine what that looks like. In one of my planning meetings with my principal and the drama teacher, I reach for a pen and a sharp pain shoots through my chest and down my arm. My principal notices and asks if I am ok and of course I say yes. See this is my first year back teaching and my winter concert must be amazing. The drama teacher who is also working with me looks at the principal and says, "No he's not. He has been in pain since around October." My principal tells me I need to go to the doctor and if I need to leave just let her know. I promised, I would go as soon as this concert was over. Truth is, I was in a lot of pain, I was walking sideways at this point, but I needed to get this concert done and it was wearing me out. We get through the concert and the parents, students, teachers, and principal are really impressed and I am good. So, I think.

We let out for winter break, Christmas comes and goes, and my gait is getting worse. So much so that my wife must help me walk straight and the pain was getting unbearable. Our church collaborates with a few other churches and we celebrate watch night services together. We combine worship teams and my wife, and I lead a few songs in worship. I hold on to the podium as I sing but no one really notices. The truth is there is so much pain shooting through my chest, arm and back that if I do not hold on to something, I might fall. Service is over and as we walk back to the car; I cannot walk a straight line at all. We go home and rest for a few hours and finally I ask my wife to take me to the ER. We arrive at the ER and wait about 45 minutes. The nurse comes to get me. My wife never lets me go by myself. She thinks I am going to leave out details from the doctor. She's right. I normally do. I tell them what has been going on and estimate how long. I am then taken back to get blood work done, MRI and CAT scan. The results come back, and the doctor tells me that my cervical is resting on my spinal cord which means any freakish move, high five, trip up, chest bump etc. and I could be paralyzed. He says I need to get surgery done before I go back to teaching. Remember, I teach pre-k through 8th grade, so I had been doing all the above from picking up the babies, to high fiving students and teachers, to playing basketball with the older students. God keeps us from dangers seen and unseen. I get two other doctors' opinions and one of them is the neurologist. He specializes in the bone and spine. This doctor looks at the same MRI and shows me where I will need to get my C1-C7 fused. All three doctors agree I need to get this surgery done before I go back to teaching. In my mind I am good financially. I am a full-time teacher with benefits. I reach out to HR and they email me all the paperwork I need. I completed all the paperwork and returned it to find out that because I had only been there for 4months

I did not qualify for temporary disability or anything else. Once my leave runs out, I am done. Did I mention that we were selling our home in Clinton and moving to St. Mary's County as well? Let me pause and thank God for a wife who knows Jesus, trusts in Him, and prays for her husband. She has an inner strength and push about her that can only come from God.

We set up the surgery for January 14th, 2019. It is delayed and rescheduled for January 21st. My wife goes to settlement on January 24th, but we have not sold the house in Clinton. In fact, we still have some packing to do and my last paycheck will be January 31st. "But my God shall supply ALL your need according to His riches in glory by Christ Jesus" (Phil 4:19). Let us talk about how He supplied ALL my needs. My concerns, ok my worries, were having a place to live while the old home was being sold; not having enough money to cover our bills for two households; not being physically able to move everything from our Clinton home to St. Mary's. We had only been at the Remnant of Hope International Church (ROHIC) for a short while. We had served at another place for over 20 years and because of "church hurt" I certainly was not going to ask them for help. Well, we did not have to. Here is what my church family did.

Francis and Janice told us that we could stay with them until I was healed enough to make the move into the new house no matter how long it took. They even gave us the code to the alarm to their home. What? God was moving on my behalf and we barely knew them. They treated us like family. I felt God changing my heart about church folks and He was using my new church family to do it. They made sure we had everything we needed. We got a chance to minister to each other as couples. God used our 27 years of marriage to minister to them. Francis and I connected and found out we both want to see God bring men to ROHIC who are on fire for the Lord and want to grow and see others grow.

Kenny and Francis told me not to worry about anything but recovering. They rallied the brothers; got a trailer and drove from St. Mary's County; moved all my boxes, furniture etc. from the home in Clinton Maryland; drove to Waldorf, Maryland packed all my boxes that were in storage; drove back to St. Mary's County and unloaded the trailer in my new home. The ladies and some of the youth of my church helped clean out the new home. Vanessa came over countless times and unpacked boxes and cleaned for a month afterward. God supplied every one of our needs. Both mortgages and utilities were paid on time; the car was paid off. We paid our tithes and had a few dollars in the bank.

Finally, we sold the house in Clinton, and we were able to pay off my student loan over 57K. Shabah! That was my other tongues. God is not finished yet. As a result of the surgery I lost my singing voice. This has been the most challenging part of the surgery. Yes, there is pain in my back, and I had to go through physical therapy to regain my balance and strength, but for me, a person who has been a singer since I was four years old and lead praise and worship for 30 plus years, not being able to sing and sound like I once did—Yeah that has been challenging. I remember sitting on my bed while recovering Staring out of the window saying, "Lord what am I gonna do? Lord, what if I never get my voice back? I can't imagine not being able to sing." I became depressed, felt stuck in the house and the enemy was working on my mind. God used The Scotts to get me focused by moving us in with them. God began to give me songs that I needed to sing, well, whistle the tunes to them. I started writing a few songs which I need to finish. God took me down memory lane and showed me how he had been keeping me all my life. He has not completed His work with my voice yet, but I have come from whistling my notes and parts to songs to now making a little more than a noise. My faith is built on nothing less, than Jesus' blood and His righteousness. Certainly, the same God who healed me from cancer, and kept me from being paralyzed, can and will restore my singing voice.

Remember, God's gotcha!! Just stand!

Pastor Margo's Heap of Hope

We see our lives in snapshots. God sees it in eternity. We see our now. He sees our entire existence. It is easy to worry, wonder, and become overwhelmed by life's sudden changes. It is easy to wonder what God is up to or question if He even sees your circumstances. Rest assured, God has a plan. Jeremiah 29:11 says, "For I know the thoughts that I think towards you, says the Lord, thoughts of peace, and not of evil, to give you an expected end." Wow! We are on God's mind. He thinks of us. The creator of the universe thinks of you. He has ideas about how to get the best outcome for you. He has a plan specifically for you. Even when your life is not going as expected for you. God is never taken off guard or surprised or trying to figure it out. His plan for you in eternity is mapped out and ends with you victorious. When you cannot figure it out and all your plans fall through, remember God is thinking of you and His master plan is in action.

The Lord also says in this verse that His thoughts are of peace and not of evil. God is not plotting against you; he is rooting for you. He is on your team. He is always working with your best interest at heart. Nothing He does is to harm you. Instead, His plans lead to you winning. His plan leads to a wonderful future and hope. He has an expected end created. His plan is to lead you there. Be confident in this, God's plan for your life is at work. Even when you are unsure if this is where you belong, God sees you right where you are. And where you are is close enough for Him to lead you. Trust His plan, it includes your win!

Elbie Williams Bio

El, as he is affectionately known, was born to Inez L. Williams and Elbie Williams, Sr. in Prince George's County, Maryland in 1968. El started singing at the young age of four and would sing to about anyone. In fact, when he was only in the sixth grade, he could sing in the Suitland High School gospel choir. While in the seventh grade El not only sang in the school choir, he sang in the Prince George's County Honors Chorus. Upon entering high school El sang in several talent and variety shows earning the title "Baby Luther." He was even invited to sing on the Cathy Hughes show where he sang *"If Only for One Night"* by the late Luther Vandross.

In 1986 El entered Bowie State University as a Music Education Major. Later he changed his major to Fine and Performing Arts where he concentrated on voice. After graduation, El spent three years teaching music in Prince George's County, four years with DC Public Schools and seven years at The SEED School in SE Washington DC.

El has sung with recording artists: Isaiah Thomas, Javon Inman, Talaya Simpson and Voices, performing in notable places such as Carnegie Hall, and the Apollo Theater. Even in this, nothing compares to his passion in leading people into an experience with God.

Contact Info.

Web: https://bit.ly/elbiewilliams

Tuesday

"Waking up in the mornings is one of the greatest gifts God can give us."

by Lisa Beverly

Tuesday

by Lisa Beverly

There is more to being married than just "being married"! When the Proposal comes along with the ring, you begin to think, "This is it! I must be the happiest woman out here!" As women, we cannot wait to call our family and best girlfriends and brag about "GETTING MARRIED". We are thinking about our dress, bridesmaids, flower girl, colors of the wedding, the venue and all that. Getting married is about the wedding, right? WRONG!! That could not be furthest from the truth. Before you say, "I do," make sure you understand what you are agreeing to because it ain't all pretty.

I met who would eventually become my husband my freshman year of high school, and he was a senior. He and his boys would lean on the wall in the hallway making inappropriate comments to all the girls as they walked by to get to 1st period. I never really paid attention to him at that time because he was a bit too macho for me. As time went on, he would ask mutual friends about me. We soon would have phone conversations and even go out a few times. There was just no spark. A couple years after graduating I became a single mother (not with him). My relationship with

Tuesday by Lisa Beverly

my daughter's father did not work out as planned. Life goes on. Nevertheless, I had always remained good friends with Will. He always was a part of my life.

I remember him picking me and my newborn daughter up from my mother's house to take us to visit one of my best friends who also was one of his cousins. He came into the house and grabbed my daughter's car seat and the diaper bag and led me to his car. Did I mention he opened the door for me? Once arriving at my friend's house, he helped me and my daughter inside and told me, "You can stay as long as you want just let me know when you're ready." He went outside to socialize with other friends and family, but still no spark. Years later we would see each other out in our community. We would speak and keep moving. He ended up having two children and getting married. I did the same. As a matter of fact, I personally handed him an invitation to come to my wedding (he did not, but his father did). A few years passed by and I did not see him, until one day he showed up to the church I was attending. He was looking sharp as a tack. I wondered where his wife was, or if he was still married or was, he like me, DIVORCED? I began to ask about him and was told he was going through some things. You know how life can be. So, we continued to see each other around town. We would speak, smile, and keep it moving.

One Friday, I stopped at a convenience store before work to get breakfast and guess who came in as I was walking out? HIM!!! Suddenly, I found myself nervous. I started to stutter as I tried to say, "How are you doing?" He gave me a smile and chuckled as I sprinted to the car embarrassed. I called my friend (his cousin) and asked her about him again, as she said, "Nah Byrd, you didn't want him back then, don't want him now." Secretly, I was mad at her, but I didn't want to seem pressed.

Now it's Sunday and the same friend called me to let me know that someone was there wanting to talk to me, and it was "HIM." We took off from there. We were inseparable. THE SPARK WAS FINALLY THERE!!!

We did everything together. We later rented a townhouse and merged our families. One day when coming home from work I walked in on something that seemed a little strange. He looked like he was "shooting up." I shouted, "WHAT ARE YOU DOING? When did you start doing drugs?" He looked at me and said, "Calm your crazy tail down. This is my insulin." I could not believe this. The only thing I could say was, "I know you're not a diabetic with the way you eat." After that I started to notice his food intake and while he was going down in size I was going up. We did not mind.

We continued with our life despite the multiple challenges that occurred in our relationship. Then one Christmas Morning when we were exchanging gifts, he nonchalantly had his daughter throw a small box in my lap. I had no idea what it was. I thought it was from her. As I opened the box, I saw it was an engagement ring. HE PROPOSED!!!!!!!!!!!!!!!!! Immediately I went to social media with my chubby finger and the ring. I called all my people to say, "GUESS WHAT YALL?!!" It was on from there. I was planning the "wedding", deciding who would do what, who would wear what, and everything that I mentioned in the beginning. It was about the "wedding" and not the "marriage." Now, a few years passed, and we moved to another county. We still were not married but working on it. My Fiancée started having medical issues more and more. He was going to the doctor every week, it seemed. We were still going forward with the "wedding" however, we decided that since we both had been married before that we did not need a costly wedding or reception. In

August (the month of our first date as adults) we decided to tie the knot. We had been through the counseling at our church and felt this was it. We called our closest family and friends the night before and told them we were getting married the next day. Almost everyone that we reached out to was in attendance. Most were happy but some wondered if I would be able to handle being married to someone with a medical condition. Let us face it we all have something going on with us. Why would I not make things right by marrying this man of God who loved me dearly. The wedding ceremony was beautiful. Just what we both wanted. I could not imagine spending the rest of my life with any other man. I felt that this man was designed for me for such a time as the time we were in. We believed that our steps were ordered. Our past experiences had led us to the altar on that day. Soon after the marriage we moved into a bigger home. One that was for us as a married couple (I's married now). Life was great. We were newlyweds for what felt like an eternity.

One day I came home from work and discovered an Oxygen sign in my new front window. I had no idea what this was about. My husband had gone to the doctor. I had spoken to him several times prior to coming home that day and nothing was said about Oxygen. I went inside to find that he needed oxygen and the tank would be here for a while. We had a deep conversation that night because I always felt like he was holding back information about his health. That night I told him that I would go with him to the next few doctors' appointments because I needed to talk to the doctors myself. Of course, he did not want that, but guess what? I was his wife *PERIODT*. I had started a new job and it was incredibly challenging, so it was difficult for me to takeoff for most of his appointments. However, I decided that it was about my baby, and I would be taking off for most of his appointments. It was at that time that I decided it was about my baby. I am glad that I went. I found out information that I would not have had the privilege of knowing.

While looking at my baby I was trying hard to hold back tears because I wanted to be strong for him. I asked him why he had not told me everything. He said, "Baby, I didn't want to worry you. I got this." He was not worried about it because God had him covered. I told him, "No, WE got this. We are a team." I remember the look in his eyes when he said, "Brown if you wanna leave, now would be the time to do it. I won't hold anything against you." What kind of person would I be? What kind of woman would I be? WHAT KIND OF WIFE WOULD I BE?!?! I reminded him what I was to him and the unconditional love that I had for him. I told him I was in it all the way, for the long haul, and I was not going anywhere. Many times, he would talk to me about him knowing that I did not sign up for this. He referred to me as being "still young" because I was in my early 40's. That was true, I was in my early 40's, however this whole thing took a toll on me. It took a toll on my body, mind, and spirit. It was extremely hard watching someone I love with all my heart suffer. As time went on some days I did not know if I was coming or going. I was working a job that was so demanding. Everyday there was craziness and foolery going on. From 8 a.m. – 4:30 p.m. I was barely making it. I remember thinking if only people knew.

Throughout the day I would talk to my husband and he would offer words of encouragement to get me through the day. He knew everyone by name. Sometimes he would call and say, "What's going on with So and So?" He remembered everything and everyone. I would sometimes think with all that he has going on how amazing it is that he still thinks of me and my trials Monday through Friday. Every Friday he would pick me up from work to start our date night. Sometimes we would stop by the grocery store or Walmart to pick up ingredients for homemade pizzas. As his illness progressed, it was better for us to have date night at home. We enjoyed each other's company. When we did go out, we had a wonderful time. When we attended family functions, he was always the life of party. He could tell a story like nobody I had ever known. When I say stories, I really mean fabrications, or shall I say, LIES? He could have you believe that he was GOD himself. That is how good he was at "fabrications." Now that I look back, I know that was his way of dealing with his circumstances. He wanted everyone around him to laugh and be happy. As time went on, he began to frequent the hospital more and more. His stays began to be longer than the prior ones. I would go to work in St. Mary's county then head up to John Hopkins when I got off. It took me two hours one way (depending on traffic) to get there and then another two to drive back home.

During that time fast food became my best friend. I was racking on the pounds and my blood pressure was always sky high. I felt like my issue could reverse but his could not. So, if he was happy, I was happy. When he would be released from the hospital after one of his stays, I tried to make it comfortable for him. I prepared meals for him before leaving the house for work so he would not have to walk up and down the stairs. I turned a vacant bedroom into a sitting room. It had two wing chairs, a TV, a small refrigerator, and a microwave in it. I did not want him to feel that he had to be confined to our bedroom. His prognosis as time went on would cause him to be confined to a bed. The doctor said it was coming, and it was sure to be sooner than we both thought. I wanted him to feel free to roam about as much as he could. I do believe that most of the time I was in denial. As a matter of fact, when he wasn't in the room, one of his doctors told me that I was in denial. They tried to prepare me for his reality.

Many times, I asked God why, and I wanted an answer. I started to struggle with my faith. I wanted to know why He would Bless me with this man and then put US through all these changes. I say, "US" because we were one unit. If one of us is suffering and hurting, we both are suffering and hurting. At night when he could not sleep because of the excruciating pain, I could not sleep because of his pain. I felt guilty trying to sleep knowing that he could not. I took on the role of trying to protect him from "outside." I wanted to intercept anything that would make him unhappy. You see, when he was unhappy, I was unhappy. The public only saw DoRight, Jr, J.R., Will, or daddy, but I saw the man that was declining right before my very eyes. I saw the brother that had difficulty taking a shower or needed help in the bathroom. I saw the brother that could not dress himself. I saw the brother that tripped over everything (when nothing was there) while trying to brace for his fall. I remember him hollering and saying, "Brown you gotta move your shoes." I started to go in and say what shoes man, but I did not because I knew it was only his frustration. Instead, I told him I would do better, and we both fell out laughing. That was the kind of relationship we had—full of jokes and laughter. We had to laugh our way through the tough times.

One day I took him up to an appointment at John Hopkins, and on our way back we wanted to stop to get something good to eat. This was always a treat after a long day at John Hopkins. We argued about where to eat because at that time I had become a professional eater. I knew all the good places to get the grub at. In Bowie, there are tons of good restaurants, but when I saw the IHOP, I said, "That's where I wanna eat." Of course, he did not want to eat there because we could have eaten at the one near where we lived. Plus, I would have to make a U-turn. Oh well, that is what I wanted, and that is where I was going. If you knew my husband, you knew at this time homeboy was pouting. I did not care though, because I was getting my breakfast food, and I wanted to be happy. That was my reasoning. Remember, I was addicted to food y'all, and if I wanted it, I was going to get it. Now, we are walking into IHOP (one of us happier than the other).

We ordered our food and began conversing when he noticed a woman with a mobile scooter. It was just like the one he had been eyeballing in a book. It would help him to get around better. It was out of our price range at the time, but we could always dream. Anyway, he stared and stared at this scooter and the owners until finally he decided to strike up a conversation with the couple. We talked to the Mercers for the next hour or so. I kept looking at my husband, speaking with my eyes saying, "Will you leave them people alone?" As a matter of fact, I texted him and said, "WILL YOU PLEASE SHUT UP and leave them alone!" He texted back a smiley face. I LOVE HIM. All this was right at the table. A few minutes later Mrs. Mercer asked if we had time to follow her and her husband to their house in Crofton. We were both like, "HUH?" They seemed like nice people and all, but I was not too keen on driving to their house. We had just met them. We both looked at them and before we could say anything the wife said, "I have a gently used scooter at the house that I would like to BLESS you with." She said that she had been waiting for the perfect person to give the scooter to, and she had met him today. We headed over to the Mercers in Crofton. We stayed for a moment laughing and talking. Her husband helped us put the scooter in the car and off we went. We could not stop by any other stores. We had to go straight home because my husband wanted to play with his new toy. I honestly believe that our steps were ordered by going to the IHOP that day. Look at GOD!!!!!! HE SURE DOES WORK IN MYSTERIOUS WAYS.

Will used that scooter for everything. I decided to work on my weight, and he was right there with me. He would take the scooter out and ride alongside me. At times he would encourage me to pick up the pace and all I could do was side eye him. I won't even tell you what I would say to him, but boy did he not get a kick out of it.

As we continued with our day to day life, my husband would become weaker and weaker, still trying to mask it with humor to the outside world. We were back and forth to the doctors appt and He was in and out of the hospital. With Christmas approaching he asked that I make sure all the children woke up at our house Christmas morning. It seemed sad to me when he asked that I reach out because they were always there for Christmas, but this time was a little different. I couldn't put my finger on it, but I knew that this time was different. All the children were home for Christmas, and I remember being upstairs crying, but did I not know why. I had to pull it together not only for him but the kids too.

We had a wonderful Christmas 2015. I decided to take a motivational class called, *The Push*, because I felt like I needed something to help me to cope better. I wanted something to do for myself outside of working and appointments. I wanted to be made whole again. Life had just kicked the life out of me. I felt that I was not living, I was just existing. I had stopped working out, so I was just feeling miserable. I talked it over with my husband, and he was so supportive. He encouraged it. He could see the toll life was taking on me. Even throughout his own sickness he always had a way of bringing light into my life.

Well, I started taking the class with a friend of mine, and it was life changing. It forced me to look at myself and why I feel the way I do about certain things. It was good for me. On January 1st, 2016, I woke up to Will looking a little different than normal. I knew the night before was not good because of the pain he had been in. We were scheduled to host a New Year's Brunch at our house that day. That was something that we did about every New Year's Day. Family and friends would come over and we would just have a good ole time laughing, joking, and eating (cannot forget that). When I looked at him that morning, I asked him if he wanted me to call everyone and let them know that we were not going to be able to host this year because he was not feeling well. He had taken on a different look. His skin had turned yellow. I thought we should have headed to the hospital. He told me NO! He wanted to go forward with our plans to host. It was like he just wanted to be around family. We went on with our day.

He sat in a recliner with a coat on because he felt it was cold in the house. Different family members asked if he was ok and why was his skin so yellow? All I could say was that I did not know, and we would be going to hospital later that day or the next day per him. After everyone left, we were both exhausted. I asked if he was ready to go and he said, "No, let us wait till tomorrow." Tomorrow morning came and I was ready to go. I asked what time we were leaving, and he did not know. He told me that he wanted to go downstairs to eat a bowl of Mannow's Soup that a friend of mine had her aunt to make (thank you so much Mrs. Christine). He ate that soup like it was his last meal. After he finished the soup, he walked up the stairs rubbing the rail every step of the way. It was like he felt he would never touch it again.

We headed to our local hospital where now they knew him by name. They ran tests. We sat for a while then out of nowhere he said, "Brown don't you have class tonight." He remembered the class I was taking. I believe it was the last class too. I was emotional because I knew I had class and I would not be able to attend. He insisted that I go to the class and come back because he was going to be there a while. I felt guilty, but he told me I should not, so I went to the class. It was not beneficial that night for me, because I cried all the way to class and all the way back.

During the class I felt sad because he was suffering. He played it off, but I know that he was afraid. I could feel it. By the time I arrived back maybe two hours later, they told me he was going to be transferred to John Hopkins. That was understandable because that is where all his doctors were.

On January 3rd, 2016, my husband was admitted to John Hopkins in Baltimore, Maryland. I traveled that road as much as I could. I spent every weekend there. On Friday when I got off from work, he was calling to see what time I would arrive. I was excited to see him. Sometimes if I had time, I would make food to take up for him and the nurses. They loved my chili. I would stop by Krispy Kreme to pick up doughnuts for the staff because homeboy had become a pistol. The nurses would call my phone to ask me if I could make him do as they asked. He was difficult at times because he was so tired. He wanted to come home.

As January was ending, I could tell it was taking a toll on him just from his appearance. He would tell me that he was starting to feel like he was going crazy. Can you imagine that? He has been in the hospital a month now. This man was not even 50 years old. However, we were planning his 50th birthday party for him straight from his hospital bed. We just knew by March he would be on that scooter scooting his way into his party.

The weekend of February 14th (Valentine's Day) he was still there. Valentine's Day had always been a big deal to him. He would surprise our daughters at school and work with balloons, candy, and flowers. He would go out of his way for his mom and me. So, this year I made him the focus point. I decorated his room and brought his favorite meal and we drank apple juice (his favorite) out of dollar store wine glasses. When I got there, he was not in his room. He was doing some testing, and by the time I saw him he was so weak. So weak that I had to walk out while they got him situated in the bed. He drank the juice but was not feeling the meal. He did not have much of an appetite.

During the previous week, the doctors told me they were going to have to put him in a Nursing Home for rehab. So, when I saw him, I remember thinking he was not ready to leave here. Even though it had been about 45 days he was not ready. We had talked wholeheartedly that weekend about our life together and he thanked me for being his wife and hanging in there with him. I was shocked and emotional at the same time. This is the man I have waited for!!! I thanked him for being a great husband to me and a father to my daughter (many did not know that he was not her biological child). I thanked him for all the good times AND THE BAD TIMES. Especially all the bad times that got us to the place we were in. We were in a good place. We loved each other with our total beings. After the moment of reflection, I looked over at him and said, "What are we doing"? It was like we both knew but we really did not know. I continued with his bath and we laughed and horsed around. Just as I was putting on the finishing touches one of his doctors came in. He wanted to talk about what would be the next plan of action in his care. The doctor said just what I had been thinking. He said that he was not strong enough to go home and the nursing home is going to be his next stop. I was to find one that could get him to dialysis. I worked at one and they were good with physical therapy, but I didn't know if it would be a good idea for him to be at the same facility that I worked at. All that was going through my mind. The doctor told him that they wanted to run more tests on him first. I shouted out "Ok! Let us do what we need to do. Let's do the test." It was at that same time when my husband shouted NO!!! And he meant that!!!! He looked at me and said he was NOT DOING ANOTHER TEST, AND HE WAS GOING HOME ON TUESDAY. Well, at that point I knew he wanted me to take a back seat and sit down somewhere. I heard from his eyes, SHUT THE HELL UP!! So, I did just that…I shut the hell up. The doctor left, and he reminded me that I was not the person that was having to go through all the testing. He reminded me that he was exhausted and no matter what happened, he was going home on Tuesday. Then he asked, "What's up with my party?"

I didn't know if I should speak, but before I could get a word out, he said, "Don't spend another dime." He no longer wanted a party. At that point I was about to break down. I felt I needed to head out of his room and admit myself into a psychiatric unit. I could not take it. At the time, I wanted him to do everything the doctor said. My emotions were already all over the place, and on top of this he did not want us to celebrate him turning 50?!?! He had been through so much, and it would be a blessing for him to see March 15th, 2016. We were going to party like rock stars. But he did not want it. I stepped out to get my composure. I thought about what he needed versus what I wanted. I went back in with a different heart. Since he was not eating any of the food I brought in, I decided to take him on a date. It was still Valentines. He had always done the most for us, so I was going to do the most for him. Now, remember I had already gotten him ready for the day. He was looking sharp as a tack in that hospital gown. I told him that we were on our way out. I was taking him to one of the cafes at the hospital. He had been complaining of being cold, so I thought soup would be good. I wrapped him up in blankets, put him in his wheelchair, and off we went. As we were going past the gift shop, he asked me if I had his bank card. Well of course I did, but I wanted to know what he needed. He told me that he wanted to take me in the gift shop so he could get me something for Valentine's Day. He reminded me that he had not had a chance to get me anything because he had been in the hospital for so long. Now y'all know I was about to lose it. At this point I had no make-up on from crying earlier, so you know I was a sight. I softly told him "I'm good baby, you are the only gift I need." I felt a breakdown coming. The tears were about to flow. Then I had to break that up and I said, "Anyway I spent all your money." We both laughed but he still tried to side eye me as he looked back (still wondering about his money, I bet. LOL). I could not let that happen because he would see my emotions were all on my face.

We finally made it to the café. We both had soup. I do not remember what kind though. The only thing I could remember was he was too weak to feed himself. So, I fed him and as I was feeding him, I was talking to

GOD the whole time in my mind asking for strength. I had kind of been at odds with God anyway because I could not understand why. Why were WE going through this? I told God we are at a good place in life and things are finally falling into place. I pleaded with God not to take him away from me. I finally have the man that you designed just for me and I wanna keep him!! He is mine. But was he really? All of this was playing in my mind as I fed him the soup. He was too weak to blow it, but he could tell when I did not blow it enough and he made me aware of that fact. Shortly after we finished our soup, he was ready to go back to his room and ready for me to leave because it was getting late. I did not want to, but I had to. The weather report was calling for snow and I was about two hours from home. Did I mention I was driving "his" car, and I am sure that had something to do with it—as I'm not the best driver.

As I was preparing to leave, I just had a crazy feeling. I remember gathering up my bags, curlers, and his dirty clothes, so I could bring them back on my next visit. Right before leaving, his favorite nurse came in with a new list of duties for him to do. I did not want to hear it because it was not going to be pretty for her. I blew him a kiss and was on my way. When walking in the halls his aides and the housekeeping staff would hug me because I was crying. I just knew something was not right. I called my mother and said, "This time feels different." She told me that I always felt like that when I left the hospital. No, not this time. It felt kind of eerie. As I drove home, I did not turn on the radio because I didn't want to hear anything but God. I prayed and drove, drove, and prayed. I knew he was not going to call because he needed sleep. We agreed that he would call once he woke up to see if I made it home safely.

I finally arrived at my empty house and started to prepare for work the next day. I was extremely tired because I never rest when I'm at the hospital. Once I was all settled, my husband called to see if I made it home safely. We talked for a brief minute before I heard his favorite nurse come in and say, "Come on Mr. Beverly, she just left now, don't be difficult." I wondered why he was up there showing off. I told him to get off the phone and do what they needed him to do. Before hanging up his last words to me were, "Are you good?" I told him I was, and he repeated it. "Are you sure you're good?" I told him I was, and we said, "I love you." After that I never spoke to him again. That was on Sunday night. In the wee hours of Tuesday morning, my husband went HOME. He did just what he said he was going to do. He went home on Tuesday.

Will now shares his home with Jesus Christ. He is still with us all in Spirit, but he is resting now. While most of us think marriage is about the wedding, it is not! It is compromising, being there for each other in all the good and bad times. It is more than the marriage certificate. It is more than having a license to have sex whenever you want it. When the vows say, "in sickness and in health" you better know just what that means. There is not one day that goes by that I am not thinking about him. I still am BLESSED!! It was a blessing to have been in his life as his wife. It was truly an honor. It was a blessing to be there for him and with him throughout the most trying years of his life. I am so grateful to God for placing him in our lives. He touched so many people in so many ways. We struggled, trust me, but in the end it was worth it. Now that's real talk.

My life now as a widow is about me trying to find my place, wanting to know where I fit in. I have days where I just want to lay around and do nothing. I do not want to complain too much because a lot of people feel

I should be over it—if that makes any sense. I get asked the question if I would ever marry again and the answer to that would be, "Yes." I have met some interesting individuals since his death, and I have kept my options open. In the meantime, I will continue to make a "better me" and continue to live my life. Waking up in the mornings is one of the greatest gifts God can give us. I plan on living life to the fullest.

Pastor Margo's Heap of Hope

Love is patient, kind, and endures among other things (I Corinthians 13). To love and be loved is a great feeling. To fall in love and get married is the dream of many young girls and women. We grow up watching Cinderella and imagine someday we will have our own prince. But married life is not a fairytale. It is not the pictures illustrated in most story books. Marriage has ups and downs, turns, and adventure. The wonderful thing about it is doing it all with a person you love. Love covers. Love goes beyond goosebumps and rose petals, love NEVER fails. Love is action. Love is unselfish and hopes. Love endures ALL things.

If you are married, hold tight to your spouse. Let the trials of this life draw you closer together. Reach for each other in difficulty. Do not isolate or pull away, pull together. Cherish time. Cherish the opportunity to be loved and share your heart with someone. Honor your vows and love uninhibited. Christ modeled this to us. While we were imperfect (with sin) He died for us. His love was not just expressed in words. He did not throw around empty promises. We were worth more than lilies to Him. He did not just capture our hearts; He captured our souls. He is the lover of our souls. Use His example to love, love again, or love harder. Love never fails.

Lisa Beverly Bio

Lisa Beverly-Brown was born and raised in Calvert County, Maryland. Lisa is the proud mother of one daughter, DeAndrea, and was blessed to have two bonus children, J.R. and A'daytra. Lisa passionately loves music especially classics like Betty Wright and Clarence Carter. Music speaks to her soul as Betty talks about "no pain no gain" and Clarence "being in my neighborhood." Lisa's close friends and family would call her an "old soul."

She also loves cooking and baking, with her masterpiece being her famous lemon pound cake. In her spare time, she diligently serves the Lord writing biblical drama skits and plays, a ministry of art and heart! She is both the playwright and often a member of the cast. In the real-world Lisa would easily admit to being "a bit dramatic" in her starring role of "life." She writes with intentional messages and added humor. She believes that is the spice of life. Lisa's love of the Lord and His service are what she aims to put on display as an active member of The Remnant of Hope International Church. She proudly serves in the women's ministry as well. In her challenging work life, she is a Staffing Coordinator by title; and a friend, confident, counselor who introduces the "Way Maker" to hurting coworkers. Her driven focus in life is to be of service to others and serve God.

Contact Info.

Web: https://bit.ly/lisabeverly

Hope Anchors the Soul

by LaKesha L. Williams

It will lead to an opportunity for your testimony.

Luke 21:13

Psalm 22:22 says, "I will tell of Your name to my brethren; In the midst of the assembly I will praise You." David would praise God in the assembly because his private deliverance deserved a public testimony. God wonderfully delivers us in the quiet moments when we are hurting, and we must be prepared to offer public praise for His care.

Are you feeling hopeful? You just read the testimonies these amazing men and women who endured some of the hardest tests and emerged to share their stories with the sole purpose of giving you hope. These men and women are simply honoring the Lord by bearing witness to His work in their lives.

The Lord commends sharing testimonies throughout His Word, particularly in the Psalms. We continually read of the Psalmist promising to tell of the greatness of the Lord "in the midst of the congregation." Often, he asks the Lord to deliver him so that he can testify of God's salvation.

The Bible is filled with the most powerful stories we will ever read or hear, but it isn't just a storybook! It is God's testimony to each of us. Now we are all part of God's story. If you have never accepted Jesus Christ as your personal Lord and Savior, you are the reason that He sent His Only Begotten Son to Calvary over 2000 years ago! If you are a believer, then you are also a part of God's story. As Christians we are to repeat the story of God's love to others who need to hear it. That includes the nations around the world, the neighbor across the street and every person like you who will read this book.

Let's stop and talk about what accepting Jesus Christ as your personal Lord and Savior looks like, and if you don't know Christ this is where you can begin a relationship with Him, right here, right now by praying the Prayer of Salvation!

PRAYER OF SALVATION

Confessing Our Sin

When we pray the prayer of salvation, we're admitting that we've sinned. As the Bible says of everyone, save Christ alone: "For all have sinned, and fall short of the glory of God" (Romans 3:23, NASB).

Some sins seem bigger than others because their obvious consequences are more serious. Murder, for example, seems to us to be worse than hatred, and adultery seems worse than lust. All sins make us sinners, and all sin cuts us off from our Holy God. All sin, therefore, leads to death because it disqualifies us from living with God, regardless of how great or small it seems. Don't minimize "little" sins or overrate "big" sins. They all separate us from God, but they all can be forgiven.

To sin is simply to fall short of the mark, like an arrow that does not quite hit the bullseye. The glory of God, that we fall short of is found only in Jesus Christ. Second Corinthians 4:6 (NKJV) says, "For it is the God who commanded light to shine out of darkness, who has shone in our hearts to give the light of the knowledge of the glory of God in the face of Jesus Christ."

The prayer of salvation, then, recognizes that Jesus Christ is the only human who ever lived without sin. Second Corinthians 5:21 (NASB) says, "He made Him who knew no sin to be sin on our behalf so that we might become the righteousness of God in Him." When we trust in Christ, we make an exchange — our sin for His righteousness. Our sin was poured into Christ at His crucifixion. His righteousness is poured into us at our conversion. This is what Christians mean by Christ's atonement for sin. In the world, bartering works only when two people exchange goods of relatively equal value. But God offers to trade His righteousness for our sin—

something of immeasurable worth for something completely worthless. How grateful we should be for His kindness to us.

Professing Faith in Christ as Your Savior and Lord

With Christ as our standard of perfection, we're now acknowledging faith in Him as God, agreeing with the Apostle John in John 1:1-3 (NASB), where it says, "In the beginning was the Word (Christ), and the Word was with God, and the Word was God. He was in the beginning with God. All things were made through Him, and without Him, nothing was made that was made." When God created, He made something out of nothing. Since we are created beings, we have no basis for pride. Remember that you exist only because God made you, and you have special gifts only because God gave them to you. With God you are something valuable and unique; apart from God you are nothing, and if you try to live without Him, you will be abandoning the purpose for which you were made.

God could only accept a perfect, sinless sacrifice, and since He knew that we could not possibly accomplish that, He sent His Son to die for us and pay the eternal price. "For God so loved the world that He gave His Only Begotten Son, that whoever believes in Him should not perish but have everlasting life." (John 3:16, NASB)

The entire gospel of John comes to a focus in 3:16. God's love is not static or self-centered; it reaches out and draws others in. Here God sets the pattern of true love, the basis for all relationships. When you love someone dearly, you are willing to give freely to the point of self-sacrifice. God paid dearly with the life of His Son, the highest price He could pay. Jesus accepted our punishment, paid the price for our sins, and then offered us the new life that He bought for us. When we share the gospel with others, our love must be like Jesus' — willingly giving up our own comfort and security so that others might join us in receiving Gods' love.

Some people are repulsed by the idea of eternal life because their lives are miserable; but eternal life is not an extension of a person's miserable, mortal life, rather eternal life is Gods' life embodied in Christ given to all believers now as a guarantee that they will live forever. In eternal life, there is no death, sickness, enemy, evil, or sin. When we don't know Christ, we make choices as though this life is all we have. This life is just an introduction to eternity. Receive this new life by faith and begin to evaluate all that happens from an eternal perspective.

To "believe" is more than intellectual agreement that Jesus is God. It means to put our trust and confidence in Him that He alone can save us. It means to put Christ in charge of our present plans and eternal destiny. Believing is both trusting His Word as reliable and relying on Him for the power to change and overcome. If you have never trusted Christ, let this promise of everlasting life be yours today!

Say It Aloud & Mean It Now!

Do you agree with everything you have read so far? If you do, don't wait a moment longer to start your new life in Jesus Christ. Remember, this prayer is not a magical formula. You are simply expressing your heart to God. Pray this with me:

"Father, I know that I have broken Your laws and my sins have separated me from You. I am truly sorry, and now I want to turn away from my past sinful life, toward You. Please forgive me and help me avoid sinning again. I believe that Your Son, Jesus Christ died for my sins, was resurrected from the dead, is alive, and hears my prayer. I invite Jesus to become the Lord of my life, to rule and reign in my heart from this day forward. Please send your Holy Spirit to help me obey You, and to do Your will for the rest of my life. In Jesus' name, I pray, Amen."

I've Prayed It; Now What?

If you've prayed this prayer of salvation with true conviction and heart, you are now a follower of Jesus. This is a fact, whether you feel any different or not. Religious systems may have led you to believe that you should feel something - a warm glow, a tingle, or some other mystical feeling. The fact is, you may, or you may not. If you have prayed the prayer of salvation and meant it, you are now a follower of Jesus. The Bible tells us that your eternal salvation is secure, "that if you confess with your mouth the Lord Jesus and believe in your heart that God has raised Him from the dead, you will be saved" (Romans 10:9, NASB).

Paul describes Jesus Christ as "our hope" (1 Timothy 1:1) and "the blessed hope" (Titus 2:13). Jesus not only came to bring hope. He is our hope.

We have hope because Jesus forgave us. Knowing Jesus brings contentment regardless of material possessions and joy despite difficult circumstances. Nothing can destroy this hope because it's stored in heaven where no earthly power can touch it.

"Praise be to the God and Father of our Lord Jesus Christ! In his great mercy he has given us new birth into a living hope through the resurrection of Jesus Christ from the dead, and into an inheritance that can never perish, spoil or fade. This inheritance is kept in heaven for you, who through faith are shielded by God's power until the coming of the salvation that is ready to be revealed in the last time." 1 Peter 1:3-5

Welcome to the family of God! I encourage you now to find a local church where you can be baptized and grow in the knowledge of God through His Word, the Bible.

About Remnant of Hope

At the Remnant of Hope International Church, we are challenged to LIVE better, equipped to DISCIPLE, and devoted to making a Godly IMPACT in our community and world!

We are committed to being God's heart and hands on Earth. Locally, The Remnant provides school supplies and lunch money to underprivileged students. The remnant also hosts Laundromat Takeovers, supplying free washing and drying of clothes as well as free laundry supplies at our local laundromats. Our Laundromat Takeover gives us the opportunity to bless both those in need and local businesses.

Globally, **The Remnant of Hope** is in partnership with **Mission of Hope Haiti.** The Mission of Hope exists to bring life transformation to every man, woman, and child in Haiti. We support Mission of Hope through our financial partnership.

Connect with us on Facebook **@The Remnant of Hope International Church**

Connect with us on Instagram **@TheRemnantofHope**

Hope Anchors the Soul by LaKesha L. Williams

Hope Anchors the Soul by LaKesha L. Williams

About the Publisher

At **the Vision to Fruition Publishing House**, we are dedicated to helping others bring their personal, business, ministry, and other visions to fruition. Whether your vision is a book you want to write, a business you want to start, a conference or event you want to host, a ministry you want to launch or an organization you want to start; or requires a more technical aspect like computer repairs, logo designs or web designs; we can help. **The Vision to Fruition Publishing House** is the publishing branch of **the Vision to Fruition Group**. We will help you walk through the process and set you up for success!

At **the Vision to Fruition Group** we have more than just clients, we have *Visionaries*. We provide solutions to equip others to pursue their visions and dreams with reckless abandon. Since 2017, we have published over 30 authors, several of which were Amazon Bestsellers. We would love for you to join our family of Visionaries as well!

Learn more here: **www.vision-fruition.com**

Made in the USA
Columbia, SC
24 October 2020

23397416R00134